MISREADING JUDAS

How Biblical Scholars
Missed the Biggest Story of All Time

ROBERT WAHLER

BookSide Press
877-741-8091
www.booksidepress.com
orders@booksidepress.com

Contents

Introduction

It isn't every day that something as important as the Gospel of Judas appears. Who is to say we won't see the opportunity wasted? In April 2006, the National Geographic Society, having acquired the rights to the discovery and tortured surfacing of the Gnostic story of Judas, presented it in print and on television to an eagerly awaiting world. Unfortunately, the experts chosen to analyze the text were not best suited to the task. They were a panel of nine biblical scholars and Coptic experts, mostly Christian, none of whom apparently had ever learned the essence of true mystic (gnostic) teaching. Since that fumbled attempt to introduce the Gospel of Judas, no fewer than forty-nine reports have been presented to the first two International Conference Proceedings on the Gospel of Judas, none of which has advanced the status of the research. *Still*, no one reports that Judas—not Jesus—is the "sacrifice" of "the man who bears me." The truth is that the gnostic tradition of Mastership succession was inverted in the fictional New Testament "Betrayal of Christ" canonical Gospels story. The evidence is now ours in the Gospel of Judas, the Gospel of Thomas, the Apocryphon of James, and the First and Second Apocalypses of James, nearly all coming to light within the last generation. All one needs to recognize it is these long-lost texts, an appreciation of mystic teaching, and a copy of the New Testament Gospels and Acts. The later dating of the Gnostic texts is not important. It is the gnostic, or mystic, *tradition* alone that is important.

Self-sacrifice is the essential essence of Gnosticism. The Gnostics of the time of the Gospel of Judas practiced self-sacrifice. There is a transformative Judas in the Gospel of Judas. There is no betrayal in the Gospel of Judas storyline. The final line, "And Judas received some money and handed him over to them," concludes the scene in which Judas "hands over" Jesus to the authorities seeking him, as in the familiar biblical version of the story, only with the correct "hands over" or "delivers," not "betrays." The literal 'handing over' is not a part of the Gnostic story of transformation. Rather, this is likely an aside to the story to tie it to the canonical story of betrayal, which was obviously widely known at the time of its Coptic drafting and couldn't be left out. Either that, or it is a later Christianizing interpolation, something not unheard of in other documents of the time. In any case, the action has nothing to do with the main narrative transformation and ascent of Judas in the original Greek draft. Every scholar involved in the investigation of the Gospel of Judas, without exception, has assumed that Jesus is the one the protagonist Judas hands over at "You will exceed them all, for you will sacrifice the man who bears me" (56:20–21).[1] He is not. Jesus is answering a question from Judas in front of the other disciples, as seen in 55:24–25: "What then will those who have been baptized in your Name do?" Judas is told that he will sacrifice his individual self to become one with his master through the mystic practice of the Name. "Name" is the Apophasis Logos, the Unspoken Word, the etheric presence of the Divine, accessible within to devotees in their meditation. This passage has nothing to do with the betrayal of Jesus Christ or anyone else. It is about mystic practice and esoteric union.

Jesus tells Judas that this baptism received in his Name "will destroy the entire race of the earthly Adam," meaning the lower, individual, selves of the heavenly Adamic race, the initiates of Jesus. "Tomorrow, the one who bears me will be tormented" (56:7). He isn't talking about himself! He is answering Judas's question. He means they, the disciples, will be tormented, not him! "Yet indeed I [say] to you [pl.,the disciples], no hand of a dying mortal [will fall] upon me" (55.9). Jesus is telling the disciples that he will be the one taking the blows within them and that he inside them will be unaffected by the blows. Then Jesus says that those who are not initiates and "offer sacrifices to Saklas"—the Negative Power—will die (55:12). The next three lines are unknown, as they are destroyed. Only then comes the climax passage: "You will

---

[1]   Marvin Meyer, ed. et al., The Gospel of Judas. 2nd ed. (National Geographic Society Washington, D.C., 2006), 51.

exceed the others, for you will sacrifice the man who bears me." Never changing the subject from what those baptized in his Name will do, Jesus now fully answers Judas's question.

Judas will be the one to "exceed" everyone, including his fellow disciples, in giving up his lower individual self in exchange for the original Adamic self, the Holy Spirit in the Master, Jesus. This is classic textbook mysticism. It is found in many other teachings of mystics from many traditions of the East and Near East. It is found in abundance in the Nag Hammadi Library texts from Egypt. An entire modern library of mysticism to illustrate this dynamic of replacement theology can be found at scienceofthesoul.org. One recent volume is titled simply *Die to Live*[2] by Maharaj Charan Singh, a recent Master at the Radha Soami Satsang Beas, in Beas, India. Please note that in deference to the Eastern tradition, 'Master' will from now on in this work be capitalized.

Do Western scholars not read Indian mysticism? Is there no awareness in the ivy-covered academic halls of the long and storied tradition of the Eastern mystics? These teachings have come to us over the last five centuries, at least, from such luminaries as Kabir and Nanak. These teachings can bring to the fore the real meaning of ancient texts like the Gospel of Judas, and yes, illuminate the books of the New Testament.

In addition to leaping to the conclusion that the "man who bears me" must be Jesus Christ, scholars have assumed that the "someone" replacing Judas in 36:1–3 in the Gospel of Judas must be Matthias from Luke's Acts 1. Matthias is not mentioned in the Gospel of Judas, and he should have been if he is a replacement for the one to "sacrifice" the Master. In fact, even in the New Testament, Matthias is not mentioned before this one occurrence or after, in Acts. He is a creation for the moment. Newer translations have "someone else will replace you, in order that the twelve 'elements' may again come to completion in their god," which is not related to Acts 1 at all. Instead, it is about the disciple Judas coming to completion in the fullness of the original

---

2   Charan Singh, Die to Live (Radha Soami Satsang Beas, Beas, India, 1979).

man, Adam. The "twelve realms of the twelve lights" (49:19) are part of the created world of Yaldabaoth, the under-god of Creation. Judas merges with "someone"—his Master, Jesus—here in 36:1: "In order that the twelve *elements*" of these lower levels of his being may reunite with their source in the "twelve realms of the twelve lights." The canonical Gospel tradition of disciple replacement is not the original tradition; the Gnostic one of replacement of self is. The canon tradition was derived, not the Gnostic one. This dynamic is well documented as parallel teaching in other mystic systems, available in various volumes at the library mentioned above. How do we know that the remake is Luke's and not the Gnostic version of the story? Because no Gnostic would ever borrow from a story of human sacrifice to illustrate their teaching. If the Gospel of Judas makes one thing clear it is this: they abhorred the sacrifice of others, particularly humans. Certainly, they would never think to sacrifice their own Master! In addition, there are several specific changes in the succession story when transformed into the betrayal story that show the order of composition, and that order is the Gnostic version first and the canon second. These will be shown in the Gnostic text analysis section to follow.

It is the contention of this author that the sacrifice of Judas in the Gospel of Judas reflects an original tradition of self-sacrifice by the Gnostics of the time, which was adopted and inverted by the proto-orthodoxy of the early Pauline church to hide that there was a successor Master: James the Just. This was the only reason for the composition and collating of the New Testament canon. The canon is therefore disinformation, not information. Its sole purpose was to hide the real Masters of the time, not to disseminate information about anyone. The way to read the New Testament is to separate the red-letter quotes of Jesus from the narrative text. Even then, the red-letter needs to be vetted for orthodox corruption with mystic understanding as a control. The red-letter is, for the most part, inspired text; the narrative Gospel author portions are not. The thought of a Master is evident in the quotations of "Christ." Just who that is remains unknown but is likely to be James himself. The epistles, or letters, can be largely ignored as

Pauline propaganda, most of them forged. Paul himself was a maverick Gnostic and a murdering liar to the end (at least in historical sources).[3] Why is he even consulted? No further progress in biblical studies will be forthcoming without this approach. The Gnostic discoveries, the Dead Sea Qumran discoveries, and an understanding of mystic teaching demand it. There are three principle sources of support for Judas as "the sacrifice" and as the cover character for the successor James: the Gospel of Judas itself, the Nag Hammadi texts of the Gospel of Thomas and the Apocalypses and Apocryphon of James,[4] and the New Testament Gospels and Acts. We will look at each in turn as each relates to the "betrayal of Christ" in all four of the canonical Gospel inversions of the succession story. The New Testament evidence for the cover-up of James as the successor is wrapped up in Chapter Three.

Christianity's unquestioning acceptance of the Holy Bible as supreme spiritual authority has been humanity's all-time biggest failing. It is now time to remedy that.

---

[3]

[4]   James Robinson, ed., *The Nag Hammadi Library* (Brill, Leiden, The Netherlands, 1978).

I

The Gospel of Judas

"Even when all the experts agree they may well be mistaken."
—Bertrand Russell (1872–1970)

No one, whether scholar or lay person, has presented the correct reading of the Gospel of Judas until now. The reason is that Western education is sorely lacking in the teaching of mysticism. Mysticism is the field of esoteric or spiritual teaching concerned with direct personal experience of the spiritual, or the Divine. The ultimate goal of mystic meditation is to merge oneself with God. No intervention is needed, no priesthood. Gnostics were mystics. Salvation from self *to union* with the Father was attained through mystic practice of His Name, or the esoteric Word, "who is the Son," not by any sacrifice of His.[5] God is not so limited that He needs to sacrifice someone so that others may live. And Gnostic texts must be read as the mystic teachings that they are, not as an offspring or development *from* orthodoxy.

Judas as "the sacrifice" and as successor James the Just in the Gospel of Judas

Dr. Lance Jenott has one of the latest translations of the Gospel of Judas, so that is what will be referenced for presenting this text. It is universally agreed that the Gospel was originally composed in Greek and then translated into Coptic, before English. We will examine selected passages to rectify incorrect interpretations given by scholars.

---

[5]   Robinson, *The Nag Hammadi Library.* 49

Where improvements are necessary, they will be noted. Additions or changes to the text are in [brackets]. Having a copy of the Meyer text and fragments (online) or Jenott's book[6]at hand is advised.

The Gospel of Judas begins on page 33 of the Codex Tchacos;[7] hence the notation of page 1 as 33. It concludes on page 58, so it is only 25 pages long.

33:1–6: "The secret discourse of the proclamation in which Jesus spoke with Judas Iscariot [the Word which is Unspoken, given to Judas by Jesus] during eight days prior to the three days before he kept Passover." The Coptic term for "secret discourse of the proclamation" is "Apophasis Logos," Greek loan words meaning, literally, "that word which is said without saying." It is the self-evident expression of the mystic Word, or "Name," of the Lord. It is "spoken" only in the metaphoric sense. It is imparted spiritually from Master to disciple. So much of the mystic message in spiritual writing is expressed in metaphor. If only Western readers would bear this in mind always! These are difficult concepts for us to grasp in even the best of circumstances—under the guidance of true mystics. Try to see beyond the words to the ideas and subtle truths that the authors sought to explain. The Apophasis Logos is the Name of the Lord. He is Word. This is the aspect of His Being that brings about salvation through "gnosis," or personal "knowing" within one's being. This has nothing to do with the written, or even the "spoken," word.

33:6–14: "When he [Jesus, the Apophasis Logos] appeared upon the earth, he performed signs and great wonders for the salvation of humanity. While some were walking in the path of righteousness and others were walking in their transgressions, the twelve disciples were called." Early mention of "passover," "sign," "walking," and "twelve disciples" all figure in tying this Gospel to the canonical 'Betrayal' and the Nag Hammadi gnostic Apocalypses of James, covered in Chapter Two.

---

[6]   Lance Jenott, *The Gospel of Judas* (Mohr Sieback, Tubingen, Germany, 2011).

[7]   Meyer, *The Gospel of Judas* 29.

33:15–18: "And he began to speak with them about the mysteries above the world and what would happen up to the end." This means the end of their lives, not the end of the world. The world will not end anytime soon.

33:18–21: "On a number of occasion she did not show himself to his disciples, but rather as a child they would find him in their midst." This is not correct. Meyer is correct to note "hrot" may be a form of the Bohairic Coptic word "hort'f" for "apparition."[8] Jesus appears in spirit form in meditation to his disciples "within them," not "in their midst" as a group. Mystic visionary experiences are internal and normally individual.

34:15–17: "Indeed I say to you, no race of the people among you will know me." The disciples are told by Jesus that they are not performing the correct "pious observances" and therefore will not be able to see the inner astral form of the Master.

34:25–35:1: "Your god who is within you and [his stars] have become contentious with your souls." The lesser god of the disciples, Yaldabaoth, is the one within them, and his astral minions (first heavenly aeon or region) are struggling for the attention of their minds.

35:2–5: "Let the [stable or 'focused'] one among you people bring forth the perfect human and stand before my face." This is the first reference to the "perfect human," or inner Master, who will reappear again at the climax of the text, as well as on the next page as the "someone" replacing Judas. "Stand" is a Qumranism for righteousness.[9]

35:10–21: "He [Judas] could stand before him, but not look into his eyes; instead he turned his face away. Judas said to him, 'I know who you are and whence you have come. You have come from the immortal realm of Barbelo, and he who sent you, I am not worthy to proclaim his

---

8   Meyer, *The Gospel of Judas* note 8, 30.

9   Eisenman, *The Dead Sea Scrolls and the First Christians*, 16.

3

Name.'" Judas is able to manifest the inner astral form of the Master, Jesus, within himself, but his concentration is not steady. So he cannot "look into his eyes." "I am not worthy to proclaim his Name" is referring to the Apophasis Logos.

35:21–27: "Now since Jesus knew that he (Judas) was considering something lofty [or holy], he said to him, 'Separate from them and I will tell you the mysteries of the kingdom; not so that you may go there, but that you will mourn deeply.'" "You," the counterpoint to the "perfect man" here, is the "lower self" or individual, "Judas." Jesus is telling him that this person, Judas, will have to be shed, and the process will bring some degree of consternation. It isn't exactly "so that" he will mourn or grieve, but just "that" he will. The following lines explain *why* he will mourn deeply.

36:1–4: "For indeed there is another who will take your place, so that the twelve [elements] shall be complete in their god." Originally, the scholastic team translating and interpreting the text had for this "twelve disciples." Now it is clear that this isn't a reference at all to the twelve disciples, but to the twelve elements that make up the complete human form. The idea here is to replace the lower propensities of the worldly man with the heavenly attributes of the mystic Master. Here we must undertake a brief examination of the makeup of man, as it is relevant to this ancient passage. The best way to comprehend what the Gnostics of the first century were attempting to do is to look in to what modern mystics attempt to do: ascend on the Master's Apophasis Logos to the Pleroma (see also John 1:51). Bear in mind that the terminology of modern mystics will be different and just as novel to the non-initiate.

With all due respect to a bright young scholar, Lance Jenott has the timing of this passage, and the one he says produced it, reversed. In what we will see is a persistent assumption made by scholars, Jenott assumes that the counterpart story in the New Testament canon, in this case the Acts 1 replacement of Judas by Matthias bringing the number of disciples back to the original twelve, has to be what this author had in mind in the Gospel of Judas. It does not have to be so, and it will prove difficult, if not impossible, for the Gnostic story of replacement to have originated in Acts. First of all, Matthias is not mentioned in the Gospel of Judas, and he should have been, given the curious use of the word "someone" in the passage. What's wrong with "Matthias will replace you…"? Secondly, there is no mention of the replacement of Judas in any New Testament Gospel; it occurs only in Acts, written in the second century. In fact, earlier, in Paul's letters, there isn't even any mention of Judas! It is quite possible that there was no Matthias when the Gospel of Judas was composed. Is it possible that there was no "traitor" Judas as well? We have no terminus a quo (earliest date possible) for the Gospel's composition in the original Greek, and, as noted earlier, it is possible that the final peripheral line about handing over Jesus for money was a later Christianizing gloss.

To provide some idea of what the "elements" might be, we turn to Swami Ji and his description of the heavenly stages through which the soul (Jiva) descends to this world and may then return after encountering a Master (Sat Guru). Paul refers to the first three of these in 2 Corinthians 12:2–4, and Jesus also mentions them in John 14:2. This is necessary to give the full picture of what the first-century Gnostics were addressing in the Gospel of Judas and in other texts from Nag Hammadi. Consider this our modern version of the Rosetta Stone for unpacking the teachings of the first-century Gnostics.

A succinct treatment of modern mystic teaching is found in Swami Ji's *Sar Bachan*.[10] Swami Ji Maharaj is the affectionate name given by disciples to the great Param Sant (Highest Master) Seth Shiv Dayal Singh (1818–1878), of Agra, India. The teachings are called "Sant Mat," or "Teachings of the Saints." It can be found in entirety online here: http://www.scribd.com/doc/30633238/The-Sar-Bachan-Prose-Swami-Ji-Maharaj#scribd

In the following excerpts, italics are original, and bracketed explanatory notes are my own.

---

[10]   Swami Ji, *Sar Bachan* (Radha Soami Beas, Beas, India 1964) 24-25; 31-35.

This world is perishable and so are all worldly things. The wise man is he who realizes the transitory and illusory nature of this world and all things pertaining to it, and makes best use of this body by worshiping the Supreme Being, through *Bhajan* [hearing the "Word"] and *Simran* [repetition, mental devotion, using names of the archons]. He thus derives benefit from all that the Creator, through His grace, has placed in the body, and takes that priceless jewel, the essence of all—the *Surat* (the soul) to its real abode.

1. [The soul] has descended from the highest planes of *Sat Nam* and *Radha Swami* [the Lord]. But it has become entangled here by the mind [and senses and] now has no recollection of its real home. It finds itself so faraway from that home it is very difficult to return to it without the grace of a perfect Sat Guru [Master, or "savior"].

What man should do now, is to take the *Surat* back to its source and real treasure house, *Sat Nam* and *Radha Swami*. Till this is done, one is not free from the pains and pleasures of this world....

Now, a description is given of the descent of the soul, and this will show how high and far is its Original Home....

11. The first and foremost region, which is the highest and the largest, which cannot even be called a stage or a region, is that of *Radha Swami, Anami* (Nameless),or *Alek* (Indescribable).

16. There are Five Melodies or Sounds [the "Five Seals" in Nag Hammadi's *Trimorphic Protennoia* and *Gospel of the Egyptians*] which can be made known to us by a perfect Master or *Sat Guru*. [Each region has its own distinctive Sound and its own characteristic secret—hence, "apophasis," meaning "said but not spoken." The five *Shabds*,or gnostic

"Seals," mark the five regions. It is by "riding," or attaching oneself to the *Dhun* (Sound) of each region that the soul can, by degrees, ascend from one region to another, up to the highest stage. See John 1:51, 14:31, and "Jacob's Ladder."] The ascent of the spirit is not possible in any other way, especially in this age of *Kali Yuga* [the fourth and spiritually lowest of the four cyclical divisions of time in the Hindu tradition].

18. Like the six superior or heavenly regions from *Sat Lok* down to *Sahasdal Kamal* [depending on whether or not vast Sat Lok is even considered to be a "region"] there are six lower or physical regions below them in *Pinda*, which are in reality reflections of the heavenly regions. [All of them relate to *Pinda,* or the physical body, while the six superior regions are related to *Brahmand*—the heavenly regions—and beyond it. These are the twelve "regions," or "twelve realms of the twelve lights," in which reside the twelve "elements" of Judas in the Gospel of Judas 36:1–3 and 49:19.]

Now, with a modern mystic perspective in mind, we can return to the Gospel of Judas:

36:11–17: "When morning came, he appeared to his disciples, and they said to him, 'Teacher, where did you go and what did you do after you left us?' And Jesus replied to them, 'I went to another great and holy race [the Adamic generation in the highest heaven].'" Bart Ehrman, Professor at UNC, Chapel Hill, says that the reason Jesus was "betrayed," or handed over, by Judas was so that he could be freed from the constraints of his physical body.[11] This passage, as Karen King and Elaine Pagels point out, is proof that he didn't need the help.[12] This is

---

[11]   Bart Ehrman, *The Lost Gospel of Judas Iscariot* (Oxford: Oxford University Press, New York, 2006), 96.

[12]   Karen King and Elaine Pagels, *Reading Judas* (Viking, New York, 2007), 135.

a major flaw in the consensus faction's reasoning for why Jesus had to be "sacrificed" according to Gnostic reckoning. The consensus faction of scholars, Bart Ehrman, et al., is set against the "revisionist" faction, led by Louis Painchaud and April DeConick—arguing for the "good Judas" and the "bad Judas," respectively. There really is no scholarly 'consensus.' There is a split.

36:17–37:16:"His disciples said to him, 'Lord, what is this great race that is more exalted than us, and holy, *and not in these realms* [italics added— proof that Jesus is not constrained by physical limitations of his body]?' Now when Jesus heard this he laughed and said to them, 'Why are you pondering in your heart about the strong and holy race? Indeed I say to you, no one born of this realm will see [that] race; nor will any angelic army of the stars rule over that race; nor will any mortal human offspring be able to join it. For [that race] is not from[…].But it is from the race of [the great] people […], powerful authorities […], nor any powers [of the realms] in which you are the kings." In spite of the lacunae, this is clearly the 'race' of the exalted redeemed.

37:21–44:14: The disciples relate a vision they have seen, and the scholars who have interpreted this are, for the most part, correct. Jesus says the ones they see debasing themselves and sacrificing animals are themselves— archetypal stand-ins for the apostolic church leaders that the Gnostics opposed. The "pillar of fire" that "falls quickly" (42:19) is in reference to the Mosaic passage in Exodus, where the pillar of fire that blocks the Egyptian charioteers at the Red Sea crossing is a salvific term. Similarly, the Adamic race will thereby be made immune to ill fate. ("They will not be moved by their stars"—42:21–22.)

Exodus 14:24–25 says that "in morning watch" [3:00–6:00a.m.] "the pillar of fire and of cloud looked down upon the host of the Egyptians and discomfited the Egyptians, clogging their chariot wheels so that they drove heavily." This is an extremely deep spiritual message. According to Dr. Randolph Stone, the Egyptians are a symbol for the

8

mind, and the chariot wheels are symbolic of the *chakras*[13] (mentioned in
Sar Bachan 18–24, above). They "drove heavily" because the devotions
of the Israelites in early morning meditation overcame (clogged) their
lower energy-center desires. (Wheels, as in Ezekiel's fanciful visions
with eyes and sparks of light, are a common symbol for these subtle
internal energy centers.) The devotees were able to harness this psychic
power to allow them to cross the Red Sea of passions, thus gaining
entrance to "the Promised Land." The Master's "strong east wind"
(14:21) is an analogy for the "Pneuma," or "wind of the Spirit" (same
as in John 3:8 and the Nicodemus story of initiation). This wind holds
back the waters until all are safely across. "Thus the Lord saved Israel
that day from the hand of the Egyptians[their mind, their own desires]"
(14:30). Every detail is symbolic—as in all other Old Testament, or
Tanak, metaphoric lessons—of the devotee becoming self- realized. The
manna in the desert, for another example, collected *before dawn*, before
it could "melt", is the Logos, or Word, manifested within at the single
eye and heard by concentration with the hearing faculty of the devotee,
the *Surat*. The same pre-dawn time of day is noted in the 'walking on
water' metaphor for meditation in Matthew ("Fourth Watch"-14:25).
In 1 Samuel 3:10, the Lord "doing a thing in Israel, at which the two
ears of everyone hearing it will [ring]" is also the hearing of the Word,
Name of the Lord, or Apophasis Logos in meditation.

42:22–44:14: "After Jesus said this he left and [took Judas] Iscariot with
him. He said to him, 'The water from the lofty mountain is [from] […]'"
No doubt, this is "from the Lord" or similar: "But it came to water the
garden of god and the [fruit] that will endure" (42:6–8). "Water" is a
symbol of the Holy Spirit, and "fruit" is the Adamic race of devotees.
"Their souls will live and they will be taken up" (42:21–23). "'Indeed
I say to you [pl.], [no ruler], no angel, [nor] power will be able to see
those (realms) that [the great], holy race [will see].' And after Jesus said
this he left" (44:8–14).
44:15–45:2:"Judas said, 'Teacher, just as you listened to all of them,

13   Randolph Stone, *Mystic Bible* (Radha Soami Satsang Beas, 1956), 281.

now listen to me. For I have seen a great vision.' But when Jesus heard this he laughed. He said, 'Why are you so worked up, you thirteenth daimon? If you speak too, I shall bear with you.' Judas said to him, 'I saw myself in the vision. The twelve disciples were stoning me. They're chasing me [rapidly].Yet then I came to the place where [I had followed] you.'" Much has been made of the reference here to "daimon." It could read either "spirit" or "demon." Some have said this belies the possibility that he is a good demon, but forever condemned.[14] It doesn't—even if the "demon" is the bad kind, as this author thinks. This is a story of a transforming Judas. He is being *"replaced by someone"*—his Master(36:1), not Matthias.

Also, Mark 14:51–52 has the "naked young man" following Jesus, being "seized" and then "fleeing." This "following" dynamic here will be of enormous significance in the canon as well as the Gospel of Judas.

The more important aspect of this passage, however, is the matter of who is doing the stoning. In all of first-century Palestine, the only figure said to be stoned by fellow disciples is James the Just. Clement of Rome in his Pseudo-Clementine Recognitions 1:70, says Saul (Paul) and company beat James and threw him from the temple steps, supposing him to be dead. The First Apocalypse of James from Nag Hammadi also has some of the immediate disciples laying hold of James to kill him. This author contends that the character "Judas" is here a stand-in for James the Just. We will see how there is much to support this contention, both from the Gnostics and from the four New Testament Gospels.

45:3–7: "I saw [a house in this place], and its size my eyes could not measure. Great people were surrounding it, and the house was roofed with lightning." Early translations had "greenery" for "lightning," which is an improvement here from Jenott. This is the region of *Sahasdal Kamal,* seen in the excerpt above from Swami Ji's *Sar Bachan.* The astral plane, the first heavenly realm, is well known for its many colorful lights. John's vision of a "heavenly Jerusalem" in Revelation is

---

14   April DeConick, *The Thirteenth Apostle* (Continuum, New York, 2007), 109 ff.

Sahasdal Kamal: "And in the Spirit he carried me away to a great, high mountain, and showed me the holy city New Jerusalem coming down out of heaven from God, its radiance like a most rare jewel, like a jasper, clear as crystal" (Rev. 21:10). Judas sees this place in his meditation and wants to be allowed in.

45:12–24: "[Jesus] responded saying, 'Your star has led you astray, Judas. For indeed, no mortally born human is worthy to enter the house that you saw. For that is the place kept for the holy ones, the place where neither the sun nor moon nor day will rule, but they will always stand in the realm with the holy angels.'" Judas will not be allowed entrance until he is a fully realized soul.

45:24–46:2: "Behold, I have told you the mysteries of the kingdom, and I have told you about the error of the stars." The "error of the stars" is the harsh fate of following the lower mind.

46:5–13: "Judas said, 'Teacher, surely my own seed does not dominate over the rulers.' Jesus responded saying to him, 'Come, and I shall [speak] with you [about the holy race—not so that you will go to it], but so that you mourn deeply when you see the kingdom with its entire race.'" This is correct, but it isn't what scholars think it is! This is saying that the old self Judas will not go to the holy race—"someone" *else* (36:1) within him will! That "someone" is 'Jesus,' *the Apophasis Logos.*

46:13–47:1: "When Judas heard this, he said to him, 'What profit have I gained by your setting me apart from that race?' Jesus answered, saying, 'You will become the thirteenth, and you will be cursed by the rest of the races, and you will rule over them. In the last days [of life] they < will---> [editorial emendation by Jenott] to you. And you will not go up to the holy race." Words are such poor conveyors of truth. They are, at best, an honest lie. "You" can mean so many things. Here it does not mean the before and after personhood of "Judas." It means the person *before* self-realization, the person Judas *was*, not the person

11

he would soon become. *That* Judas was to ascend to the holy race. It is certainly true that Judas was set apart "from" the holy generation. No one of mortal birth will ever go there. Even Jesus! Not until he became realized. Everyone, Masters included, must transfigure into their resurrected state before they can ascend. This is the way of the Masters since time immemorial. It is so *today.*

Also of immense significance to the position of April DeConick and friends regarding "the Thirteenth" is the answer Jesus gives to Judas's question: "What profit have I gained …?" Jesus immediately answers, "You will become the Thirteenth." So whatever "the Thirteenth" means, becoming it is something that "profits" Judas. The Thirteenth is good, not bad. Much debate has centered around the number thirteen and the "thirteenth realm." Being the realm of Sophia and/or Yaldabaoth, depending on the source, this can be a good or not-so-good identifier. What does it matter? If Judas "rules over" the Thirteenth realm, it means that he rules over whomever resides there—Sophia, Yaldabaoth, or whomever. This is, therefore, a reference to his exaltation.

47:1–13: "Jesus said, '[Come], and I will teach you about the [mysteries] which […] human will see. For there is a great boundless realm, the size of which no angelic race has seen. [In] it there is [a great] Invisible Spirit, whom no angel's eye has seen, nor inner thought received, nor has He been called by any name." For some inexplicable reason, "there is a great Invisible Spirit" was omitted from the 2006 *National Geographic* special narrative on television. Perhaps it was offensive to Christian censors. In any case, the Spirit, "aeon," or region "never called by any name" is none other than Sant Mat's *"Anami Desh,"* the highest realm of Eastern mystic cosmology, the "region without a name," as we saw in *Sar Bachan.*

The Prayer of the Apostle Paul:

The very first book in the Nag Hammadi Library (front flyleaf, Codex 1) is the Prayer of the Apostle Paul. In the short prayer is, notably,

"Grant what no angel eye [or "eye of any angel"] has [seen] and no archon ear [has] heard and what has not entered into the human heart which came to be angelic and (modelled) after the image of the psychic God when it was first formed in the beginning, since I have faith and hope" (A25–30). This composition draws on the Apostle Paul, where he says, "But as it is written, 'What no eye has seen, nor ear heard, nor the heart of man conceived, what God has prepared for those who love him'" (1 Cor. 2:9). Both could be reflecting on Isaiah 64:4 and 65:17, but the fact that the Gospel of Judas has "[In] it [the great and boundless realm] there is a [great] Invisible Spirit, whom angel eye [or 'eye of any angel'] has not seen, nor inner thought received, nor has He been called by any name" (47:8–13) certainly raises a question about who had this distinctive phrasing first.

47:13–18 (the Gospel of Judas): "In that place appeared a luminous cloud, and he (the Invisible Spirit) said, 'Let an angel come forth for my attendance.'" This is the luminous cloud of the Great Invisible Spirit (*Radha Soami*), which bears recalling later when Judas enters it. There is no mention that there is any other.

47:18–21: "And from out of the cloud came a great angel, Autogenes, the god of the light [*Shabd Saroop*]." It is the self-generated "self-begotten living Word, the son of the great Christ, son of the ineffable silence, who came forth from the invisible and incorruptible Spirit."[15] For the next five pages, 48–52, a complex gnostic cosmology is detailed. For our purposes, it is sufficient to note that Autogenes begat Adamas, the image of the perfect human, and he begat Seth, the father of the imperishable, kingless race of man—the holy generation—as well as the created realms of the Negative Power, Yaldabaoth, and his minion, Saklas, "the fool." These are known as the grand division of *Bramand*, ruler *Kal*, and consort *Yama*, lord of death, in Sant Mat. Angel Michael is the father of the races of man destined to be lost, whose spirits are merely on loan from God (53:22).

---

15   Robinson, *The Nag Hammadi Library* 211.

53:5–54:12: "And the angel said to him, 'The life of you and your children will be for a limited time.' Then Judas said to Jesus, '[How] long will a person live?' Jesus answered, 'Why are you so shocked that Adam and his race received his kingdom in a limited way, just like his ruler?' Judas said to Jesus, 'Does the human spirit die?' Jesus said, 'In this way God commanded Michael to give spirits of people to them while they serve, as a loan. But the Great One commanded Gabriel to give spirits to the great kingless race, the spirit and the soul. Therefore, the rest of the souls [… five lines missing here] spirit within you [pl.] which you [pl.] have made to dwell in this flesh in the races of the angels. But God had knowledge brought to Adam and those with him so that the kings of chaos and the underworld might not [lord it] over them.'" Gnostics separate humans into three groups: Pneumatics, Psychics, and Hylics. The Pneumatics are the ones destined by Gabriel in this life to become God-realized as the holy race. The Psychics are destined for it in another birth. The Hylics, the ones to whom Michael granted spirits, the worldly souls, are doomed. Each member of "the human race" evidently possesses a soul as well, yet one that is destined for obliteration at the time of bodily death (43:15–16). This is because they are not "sown" with the Word and will die, along with "perishable wisdom" (44:1–4).

54:13–55:6: "Then Judas said to Jesus, 'So what will those races do?' And Jesus said, 'Truly I say to you [pl.], the stars are coming to fulfillment over all of these. And when Saklas fulfills the times allotted to him, their first star will bring the races and the things mentioned (before) shall be brought to fulfillment: then they will [regenerate] in my name, and they will [slay] their children, and [forsaking] wickedness […four lines missing] bringing their races [their subtle and gross bodies] and offering them to Saklas.'" "First star" is Judas, as Jenott says. "Those races" are Adam's "and those with him." This has to be a positive passage. Jesus is answering Judas's question, "What will those races do?" Since "you" is plural in 54:5–6, he is speaking to all those in the

Adamic race (54:9–10), or the disciples as a group. When Saklas has finished his "allotted" time with these souls; that is, when they die, the "things mentioned before" will be brought to fulfillment (54:17–24). The things mentioned before are "stars coming to fulfillment" (line 17) "so that the kings of chaos and the underworld might not [lord it] over them" (54:10–12). This segment does not refer to the wicked priests doing horrible things. It is about the Adamic race! Jenott is completely wrong here. Judas is not leading the "future outbreak of sin that Jesus predicts will follow the completion of Saklas' time."[16] Quite to the contrary, he is leading the Adamic race to salvation as the successor! Unlike the scholars who first assigned "*fornicate* in my name," I make the first Coptic word of this phrase out to be "regenerate," without the pejorative sense of "fornicate." Whether this is even possible remains to be determined. Repeated efforts to contact scholars involved in the Gospel of Judas have proven fruitless. One of the reasons for this book is to instigate further research on some of these critical questions and to promote further debate on the correct interpretation of the text. The sense here must be positive, however. Again, Jesus is speaking about the Adamic race, not the priesthood! "Regenerating" in my Name (54:25) is a *good* thing, as it means transforming into the higher Being who is the Master in this world. It is performing devotion to the Father. Even "[slay] their children" (54:26) may be a good thing. Unfortunately, the following five lines have been lost, so it is hard to tell, but the author is still talking about the holy race at 54:5–12. This *must* be a positive reference at the last two lines of page 54. Perhaps it means the holy race will slay their desires, the "offspring" of the lower self. Even the unsaved do not slay their children, literally.

55:6–9: "And afterward, Israel will come, bringing the twelve tribes of [Israel] from [. . .]." This is a fascinating new addition from a fragment of text only recently brought to light. The first mention of Israel is to a person, obviously. The second is to the nation, or the body of believers.

---

16   Jenott, *The Gospel of Judas* 218.

The lacuna at the end of the sentence is "Egypt" (per Meyer[17]) as a symbol for the world, here and frequently so in the Bible. The "from" could well be originally "ex" in the Greek: "out from," just as in John17:12, where "none *of* them" is really "no one *out from* them" is lost, but the son of perdition [the devil *in* each one *of* them]. (This makes the idea that John here means Judas is the devil moot.) In this passage, "Israel" is taking the nation of believers *out from* the world. That means this is a savior figure, or deliverer, as Jacob was. This is where it really gets interesting: "Israel" cannot mean the Tanak Patriarch Jacob (Genesis 35:10), so who is this Israel? It says he "will come." Jacob is the Greek for Hebrew Ya'acov, and James is the English for Jacob. Is "Israel" James? The one "to come"? James is already hinted at in the vision Judas has in 44:15–45:2. Here is "Israel"—Jacob, or James—bringing "the tribes of Israel" out from Egypt, bringing the faithful out from the world. And it looks like he may well be Judas, the protagonist throughout.

55:10–13: "And all the [races] will serve Saklas while sinning in my Name. And your star will [rule] over the thirteenth realm." A "ruling star" has to be significant. Stars were a very important symbol in the ancient world. In the Dead Sea Scrolls, the prophecy of the "star" that "will arise from Jacob" in the star-and-scepter-of-Israel passage of Numbers 24:17 is central to the ethos of the Righteous Teacher and James, according to Dr. Eisenman.[18] We just saw in the fragment passage above that both "Jacob" and "Israel" pertain to James, and here we have both in the same sentence with "star of"—a powerful symbol of dominion that is to recur in the Gospel of Judas for the character Judas. In fact, two lines later, in Numbers 24, Jacob is said to "exercise dominion." This was *after* the life of the Patriarch Jacob, so it must be some other namesake. It appears that here, and in the Dead Sea Scrolls, James is associated with a ruling star.

55:15–22: "[Judas] said, 'Teacher, why [are you laughing at me]?' [Jesus]

---

17   Marvin Meyer, *The Gospel of Judas (Wipf and Stock, Eugene, Oregon, 2011)*, 35.

18   Eisenman, *The Dead Sea Scrolls and the First Christmas*, xxiv.

responded [saying], "I am not laughing [at you, but] at the straying of the stars. For these six stars go astray with these five warriors, and all of them will perish with their creations." Jesus laughs four times in the Gospel of Judas but says several times to the disciples or Judas that he is not laughing at *them.* So, the laughter is not a support for Jesus denigrating Judas. He is a human who laughs. The six stars are likely symbols here for the chakras, mentioned in *Sar Bachan,* since they consort in error with "the five warriors." The five warriors or "combatants" (the original translation from Meyer) are Sant Mat's "lust, anger, greed, attachment, and vanity." They constitute the perversions of the normal function of the *Antahkaran* (inner mind), the *Khat chakras,* the worldly or bodily centers of activity, in the Eastern mystic systems. It is these "kings" that will later be seen to have "grown weak" in Judas as he approaches mastership. They will all "perish with their creations [offspring]"—desires—as Judas grows in spiritual maturity.

Incidentally, according to Dr. Stone, Joshua 10 and the story of the five kings slaughtered without mercy by Joshua (Joshua 10:12–15) is about a battle with these five tendencies of the lower mind: Joshua fought against the five kings who symbolize the five passions of *kam* (lust), *krodh* (anger), *lobh* (greed), *moh* (attachment), and *ahankar* (vanity). These five kings he had cornered—by concentrated effort of mind energy—in the cave of Makeda, a *chakra* or center, and slew them there (God famously making the sun to stand still for about a whole day). These were the enemies of Israel, and he needed more time and light in order to conquer them. This light was given by the light of the Inner Sun [Gibeon] and Moon [Aijalon], and he went from conquest to conquest, on to the Promised Land, and Higher Regions of Consciousness.

55:23–25: "And Judas said to Jesus, 'Well then, what will those who were baptized in your Name do?'" Judas asks Jesus a direct question about baptism into the Apophasis Logos: *What will they do?*

55:26–56:6: "Truly I say [to you], this baptism [which they have received in] my Name [… three lines lost] it will wipe out the entire race of the earthly Adam.'" The "race of the earthly Adam" means the worldly man, the 'lower self' of the initiate.

56:7–11: "Tomorrow he who bears me will be tortured. Yet indeed I [say] to you [pl.,the disciples], no hand of a dying mortal [will fall] upon me." Jesus is answering Judas's question, and he addresses his answer to all the disciples (or perhaps the whole Adamic race). He is telling them what will happen *to them,* not to him! "He who bears me" is *them.* This is a generic, archetypal reference to *the ones who have taken on the Master,* not to Jesus! The "dying mortal" reference is to the uninitiated. Their hand of torture will not fall upon the "new man" who "bears" the Master.

56:12–14: "Truly I say to you, Judas, that those who offer sacrifice to Saklas [will die]." Those souls who remain outside of the protection of the Master will die unsaved. (Some will be saved in a future life).

56:15–21: "[… three lines lost] every wicked thing. But you yourself will do more than all of them: for the person who bears me, you shall sacrifice him." Another translation, from Meyer et al., is "for you shall sacrifice the man who bears me." Jenott's version may be more literal, but it is also more awkward. In any case, *it isn't about Jesus at all.* Jesus is telling Judas, in answer to his direct question about what those who are baptized into his Logos will do, that he will willingly sacrifice his own personhood in exchange for the Master's. This baptism in his Name, Jesus says (56:4–6), will destroy the earthly former self of the initiate, but it doesn't say *what they will do* (55:25). Later lines tell of how these initiates will suffer at the hands of lesser beings but not feel the blows (56:8–11). Also, Judas is told that those who sacrifice, or show fealty, to Saklas—the god of this world— will die to God, unsaved (56:12–14). "But you yourself" begins his answer to Judas's question. Here it is: Judas will sacrifice the man who bears his Master.

He will sacrifice himself. This is what Jesus tells him he will do with this "baptism in my Name." He and his Master *will become one.* Only those who give up themselves spiritually, completely surrendering body, mind, and soul to the Master, will come to know Him-who-is, the progenitor of the imperishable holy race of Seth.

The Nag Hammadi Library Sources for Support of Judas as the Sacrifice in the Gospel of Judas

Scholars seem unaware of the many similar referents in Gnostic lore to the sacrifice of self—even a reference in the New Testament! Mark 14:21 says, "For the Son of man goes as it is written of him, but woe to that man by whom the Son of man is delivered!" This isn't a betrayer and Jesus he is speaking about, but the disciple and the Holy Spirit, the Logos "delivered." He isn't betrayed! That is a mistranslation of "paradidotai." In other places in the Gospels, this Greek word is rendered as "delivered" or "handed over," such as in John 19:16. The man who delivers the Son is the lucky, diligent disciple, not a traitor. His woe is that he will cease to exist, will not "ascend to the holy generation," because his Master, the Holy Spirit within, will be all that is left. Mark and subsequent Gospel authors misappropriated this true statement by a real Master (probably James) to their own nefarious purposes. The real function of this quotation, and why it was hijacked, will be covered in detail later.

One doesn't even need to leave the Gospel of Judas to find an allied referent about sacrifice of self: 36:1–3. "For indeed there is another who will take your place, so that the twelve [*elements*] shall be complete in their god." But we will survey the entire Gnostic library to see just how often this replacement dynamic is revealed. The next tractate to have a referent is just before the Gospel of Judas in the Tchacos Codex. It is likely that the Gnostics placed their books together for a reason. The one just before the Gospel of Judas, *James,* is a version of the Nag Hammadi First Apocalypse of James. Italics have been added here, and following, to demonstrate the sacrifice of self: "Then you will attain to the One Who Is, *and you will no longer be James*, but someone who in every respect is in the One Who Is." CT 13:23–14:2. (Italics added for emphasis in all sources, this section.)

Then, going back a tractate to the Letter of Peter to Philip, we find, "As for you, *fight like this*, for the rulers fight against *the inner person*" (CT 6:1–3) and "Peter answered and said, 'He died for us, we ourselves are *to die* for humanity.' Then [a voice] came to them [saying], 'I often told you, *you are to die*'" (7:1–7). "Jesus is a stranger to death. But *we are the ones who have died* through the transgressions of the Mother [Sophia]"(8:3–5). Present in the more complete Nag Hammadi version, which was better preserved, is *"When you strip off from yourselves what is corrupted,* then you will become illuminators [within—not "in the midst of"] mortal men" (NHC 137:5–10). The Tchacos Codex text was badly damaged, and this passage was completely missing (CT 5).

The Nag Hammadi Apocryphon of James says, "Therefore become seekers of death, like the dead who seek for life; for that which they seek is revealed to them. And what is there to trouble them? As for you, when you examine death, it will teach you election [choice]. Verily I say unto you, none of those who fear death will be saved; *for the kingdom [of God] belongs to those who put themselves to death.* Become better than I; make yourselves like the son of the Holy Spirit!" (NHC Book I, 6:5–20). Also, *"woe to those for whose sake I was sent down* to this place; blessed will they be who ascend to the Father! Once more I reprove you, you who are; *become like those who are not,* that you may be with those who are not" (13:5–15). Note that "woe" is a good thing. This, of course, doesn't promote suicide. It means giving up the person you have been for the One Who Is within you. In a parallel with the Gospel of Mark 14:51–52, there is, *"I shall strip myself,* that I may clothe myself" (Apocryphon of James 14:35).

The Apocryphon of John, Nag Hammadi says, "And *I entered* into the midst of their prison which is the prison of the body" (Books II, III, and IV, Book II 31:1–5).

In the Gospel of Thomas, Nag Hammadi: logion 108 reads (italics added), "Jesus said, 'He who drinks from my mouth [the "kiss"] will become like me. *I myself shall become he,* and the things that are hidden will be revealed to him'" (II, 50:25–30). This is a parallel to "I am he" in John 13:18–19, where Jesus says he knows whom he has chosen, and then, "I am he," showing that he isn't speaking of any traitor. More on this in a later segment. In logion 61 is an enigmatic: "Two will rest on a bed; *the one will die, and the other will live....* Therefore I [Jesus] say, *if he is destroyed* [speaking to disciple Salome] he will be filled with light" (43:20–30). The "two" are obviously the one person who *was,* and the one who 'lives' now, the Master.

The Gospel of Philip, Nag Hammadi, says, "As for man, *he was offered up to God dead,* and he lived" (55:5). Then, "God is a man-eater. For this reason *men are [sacrificed] to him*" (II, 63:1–5). Also, "Those who say they will die first and then rise are in error. If they do not first receive the resurrection *while they live,* when they die they will receive nothing" (73:1–5). The resurrection is the replacing of self. Also, "The cup of prayer contains wine and water, since it is appointed as the type of the blood for which thanks is given. And it is full of the holy spirit, and it belongs to the wholly perfect man. When we drink this, we shall receive for ourselves the perfect man. The living water is a body. It is necessary that we put on the living man. Therefore, when he is about to go down into the water, *he unclothes himself, in order that he may put on the living man*" (75:15–25). "Bring forth the perfect human" is the version of this found in the Gospel of Judas (35:3–4).

The Dialogue of the Savior, Nag Hammadi, states, "Rather, I say to you that you will become blessed *when you strip [yourselves]!*" (III,143:20).

The Thunder: Perfect Mind, Nag Hammadi: "But *whenever you hide yourselves,* I myself will appear. For [whenever] you [appear], I myself [will hide] from you" (VI,16:35–17:5).

The Second Treatise of the Great Seth, Nag Hammadi: "*We shall die* with Christ" (CVII, 49:25). "It is I [Christ] who am in you [pl.], *and you are in me,* just as the Father is in you in innocence" (49:30–35). "I visited a bodily dwelling. *I cast out the one who was in it first, and I went in.* And the whole multitude of the archons became troubled.

And all the matter of the archons as well as the begotten powers of the earth were shaken when it saw the likeness of the image, since it was mixed. *And I am the one who was in it, not resembling him who was in it first. For he was an earthly man,* but I, I am from the heavens above" (51:20–30). "They [the dead in Christ]… having shed zealous service of ignorance and unlearnedness beside the dead tombs [bodies], *having put on the new man,* since they have come to know the perfect Blessed One of the eternal and incomprehensible Father and the infinite Light, which is I [Christ], since I came to my own and united them with myself" (59:1–10).

The Three Steles of Seth, Nag Hammadi: "Thou art one….For thou art the existence of the mall. Thou art the Life of the mall" (VII,125:25–30).

Trimorphic Protennoia, Nag Hammadi: "I am the Life of my Epinoia [Remembrance] that dwells within every Power and every eternal movement and (in) invisible Lights and within Archons and Angels and Demons and every soul dwelling in [Tartaros,the underworld] and in every material soul" (XIII,35:10–15). "I hid myself within them all" (49:20).

Gnostics practiced the sacrifice of self, as is shown in the dozen different Gnostic texts above, with perhaps more than three dozen selected citations as examples of self-sacrifice of the devotee for the goal of God-realization.

Judas becomes the Master in the Gospel of Judas

56:22–25:

> Already your horn is raised,
> your wrath is kindled,
> your star has [ascended],
> and your heart has [grown strong].

This ode to the transformed Judas is very beautiful and very powerful. Let's not miss it. A "horn raised" is a tribute to the victor in battle, an announcement of one's coming. Judas has conquered his mind and is now one with his Master. His "wrath is kindled" *against himself.*

The First Apocalypse of James says, "Truly I say to you that you have stirred up great anger *and wrath against yourself*" (32:10, italics added). Remember, this tractate is just before the Gospel of Judas in the Codex Tchacos. The "sacrifice" of "the man," as he was told by Jesus that he would do, is the result of his wrath against his old self. Dr. DeConick, who is no friend of Judas, has his star "ascended," not "passed by," as so many others have. Judas is now front and center. His heart has become strengthened to take over the duties of Master.

To be fair, the Tchacos Codex version of the First Apocalypse of James is different. "He has stirred up his anger and his wrath against you" is what Meyer et al., have for this passage. Perhaps this early translation was incorrect.

To see where this wrath is rightly directed, we can look at the Gospel of Mary, Papyrus Berolinensis 8502: "When the soul had overcome the third power, it went upwards and saw the fourth power, [which] took seven forms. The first form is darkness, the second desire, the third ignorance, the fourth is the excitement of death, the fifth is the kingdom of the flesh, the sixth is the foolish wisdom of flesh, *the seventh is the wrathful wisdom* [all italics added]. These are the seven [powers] of wrath. They asked the soul, 'Whence do you come, *slayer of men,* or where are you going, conqueror of space?' The soul answered and said, '*What binds me has been slain, and what surrounds me has been overcome, and my desire has been ended, and ignorance has died. In a [world] I was released from a world, [and] in a type from a heavenly type, and [from] the fetter of oblivion which is transient.* From this time on will I attain to the rest of the time, of the seasons, of the aeon, in silence'" (I, 16:1–17:5). So beautiful! Sounds like this gnostic wrath really is directed against self. All that's left now is the Master within.

57:1–5: Oh, what we would give to have the full text of these five lines, but, alas, three of them are destroyed due to poor handling. Here is what we have: "Truly [I say to you (sg.)], your final [... three lines missing ... the thrones] of the realm have been [defeated];" This is probably about the final days of Judas and how the powers of the archons that have, up until now, controlled his mind but "have been defeated."

57:6–10: "The kings have become weak; the races of the angels have mourned; the wickedness they [sowed...] is obliterated [and] the ruler is wiped out." The "kings" are, again, the five perversions of mind: lust, anger, greed, attachment, and vanity. They are overcome by meditation on the Apophasis Logos. The "races of angels" no longer have Judas to kick around because the wickedness they sowed is obliterated and the archon in charge is defeated. Judas is free.

57:10–15: "[And] then the [fruit] of the great race of Adam shall be exalted, because before heaven and earth and the angels that race exists throughout the realms." The "fruit" is the spirit and soul of the Adamic race, which Judas will now "deliver".

57:16–21: "Behold, you have been told everything. Raise your eyes; see the cloud, the light within it, and the stars surrounding it. And the leading star, that is your star." Here, "raise your eyes" means shift your attention within to the point between your two eyes, to the "single eye," in meditation. Judas sees the cloud of light and the stars (perhaps of his disciples) with his star leading his way. Since it is "your star," not "their star" or just "star," this is the star that leads *him* into the luminous cloud. Incidentally, even in the canon, when Jesus says, "Rise up, let us be going!" (Matthew 26:46 and John 14:31, for example), he means rise up *in meditation: "Watch!* The spirit indeed is willing, but the flesh is weak."

57:22–58:6: "So Judas raised his eyes; saw the luminous cloud; and he entered it. Then the people standing on the ground heard a voice coming from the cloud, saying '[...] great race [... three lines lost].' Then Judas stopped looking at Jesus." Some scholars[19] have claimed that Judas is not the one entering the cloud, but Jesus. This simply cannot be. Birger

---

[19]   April DeConick, Gesine Schenk Robinson; Madeliene Scopello, ed., *The Gospel of Judas in Context* (Brill, Leiden, The Netherlands, 2006), 87.

Pearson claims that the conjunction "and" in "Judas raised his eyes; saw the luminous cloud; *and* he entered it" means that the subject for "he entered it" can mean Jesus—an asyndeton.[20] Unfortunately for that theory, "Judas raised his eyes" doesn't mean Judas looked upward with his baby blues. It means that he focused his inner attention upon the highest energy center in his subtle spirit body, the *Tisra Til*, and raised his consciousness completely up and out of his body. Big difference! Judas thereby was able to enter the luminous cloud and become one with Jesus within. Thus Judas "stopped looking at Jesus" because they were merged *into One Being*. If only scholars would study mysticism, where might our understanding be by now?

One can see by now that a true gnostic reading can be quite different from an orthodoxy-infected one. Please, everyone, read the Gospel of Judas as the Gnostic text that it is. Stop importing a New Testament bias into it!

57:6–26: The rest of the Gospel of Judas is an abbreviated closing scene taken straight from the canonical four Gospels. It has nothing to do with the Gnostic story of Judas, which ended in the luminous cloud and with an exalted "great race" in 58:1–2. Whether a sop to orthodoxy or a later scribal Christianizing gloss, it matters not. Judas is now the Master, and Jesus is no longer Master.

Now we will turn to the most exciting news the world has ever heard: the story of the Gnostic mastership installation that was turned on its head by the authors of the New Testament Gospels to become the most famous betrayal in history.

---

[20]   April DeConick, *The Codex Judas Papers* (Brill, Leiden, The Netherlands, 2009), 148.

II

The Nag Hammadi Library

Judas is the sacrifice; that much is clear by now. But who is this character, Judas? Is he the man that Paul never mentioned, the one he never knew, just like the Jesus he never knew? The Judas that history never knew? The Judas that the New Testament called "the betrayer"? Or maybe he is someone else? The author of the Gospel of Judas is already coy about the identity of his "replacement," so maybe there is something further to be uncovered here. There are several Gnostic texts that mention Judas, but, more important than that, there are several that mention *a Successor Master.* As Dr. Robert Eisenman has so astutely pointed out, this "replacement" in Acts 1, Matthias, occurs at just the point in the dialogue that a successor to Christ should be mentioned and isn't.[21] Dr. Eisenman goes on to show the details of Judas as a cover for James the Just in Acts 1 and Stephen as a cover for James in Acts 7, during the stoning of Stephen. The present author also covers these details in another book on James.[22] The logical thing to do was to take these details on Judas and Stephen as James in Acts and go back *into the Gospels* to see whether James resides there as well. It turns out that he does—in incredibly inventive and sophisticated writing by extraordinarily clever people: the authors of Mark, Matthew, Luke, and John.

Sources with James the Just as successor savior in the Nag Hammadi Library

21   Eisenman, *James the Brother of Jesus* 166.

22   Robert Wahler, *The Bible says Saviors – Obadiah 1:21* Xlibris, Bloomington, IN, 2009), 155.

Please note: Nag Hammadi Codices book numbers and tractate numbers follow their titles in the remainder of this chapter.

The Gospel of Thomas (II,2)

Perhaps the earliest of the classic Gnostic texts is the Gospel of Thomas. It is here that we find the earliest mention of the successor of "Christ," James the Just.

The Gospel of Thomas II, 2 is an early Gnostic Christian source, perhaps as early as the genuine letters of Paul, commonly held to be the earliest valid Christian source of information about Christ, his companions, and his teachings. This is because it is not a narrative, but a record of "sayings" and preserves some of the earliest forms of New Testament Gospel teachings of Christ.

From Logion 12 comes the following: "The disciples said to Jesus, 'We know that you will depart from us. Who is to be our leader?' Jesus said to them, 'Wherever you are, you are to go to James the Just, for whose sake heaven and earth came into being.'" If this text is early, where is James in the New Testament? Does even Jesus merit such high praise as this? We will soon find James buried under a flurry of aliases and fictional creations to hide his coming—a Master in his own right, who was a threat to the proto- orthodox church. ("Who and whatever James was, so was Jesus"[23]) Any authority besides the Pauline leaders in the first-century nascent church was not welcome. It was to be the New Testament Gospels' function to hide the coming of savior James. In its literary genre, according to Helmet Koester in his introduction to the Gospel of Thomas in the Nag Hammadi Library by Robinson,[24] the Gospel of Thomas is closer to the sayings source "Q" (German for "Quelle," which means "source") than it is to the Gospels themselves. Indeed, it could be even earlier, as it doesn't include any of the sayings about the future coming of the Son of Man, so characteristic to Q (cf. Luke 12:8, 10, 17:22, 24, 26. For further comparison, several of the

---

23   Eisenman, *James the Brother of Jesus* 963.

24   Helmut Koester, introduction in Robinson, *The Nag Hammadi Library*, 124.

more original and shorter forms of New Testament parables are found in Gospel of Thomas sayings 8, 9, 57, 63, 64, 65, 96, and 109.) The Gospel of Thomas is very early, perhaps the earliest of them all. We can already see something is changed in later sources of the New Testament in how James is regarded.

The Apocryphon of James (I,2)

In the Apocryphon of James, NHC Codex I 1–16, is "The twelve disciples [were] all sitting together recalling what the Savior had said to each one of them" (2:5–10). "Leave *James* [italics added] and Peter to me that I may fill them. And having called these two, he drew them aside … lo, the Savior appeared, after departing from [us while we gazed] after him" (2:17–18, 2:30–35). "The Savior said, … 'Henceforth, waking *or sleeping* [italics added, likely meaning meditation], remember that you have seen the Son of Man, and spoken with him in person. Woe to those who have seen the Son [of] Man; blessed will they be who have not seen the man [lower self], and they who have not consorted with him, and they who have not spoken with him, and they who have not listened to anything from him; yours is life! Know then that he healed you when you were ill that you might reign'" (3:15–25). Each one of these lines has a counterpart in the canonical betrayal scene in the four Gospels. The "twelve" were sitting together (at the Last Supper); they were "sleeping" in the Garden of Gethsemane, even "not consorting with him" (they all fled and Peter "denied" Jesus) or not "listening to him" ("Will you not *watch* with me"—"watching" means meditation on the Word—"for an hour?"- Matt. 26:40–41).

The Savior "appeared after departing from us while we gazed after him," as does Jesus with Judas at the end of the Gospel of Judas, showing that they were with the Savior in meditation. They were not separated from him as he ascends in the luminous cloud as in the consensus opinion regarding the ascent scene in the Gospel of Judas. Three times Jesus "comes to them" in the "Garden" of their meditation and finds them "sleeping," or not "gazing after him." There was an admonishment of "woe to the man who delivers me" from Jesus ("he who betrays me") and a healing (of Malchus). This is just the first of the many parallel phrases showing affinity between the Gnostic original tradition and the New Testament. Many are reversed or inverted tendentiously, but not all. The order of phrases is usually similar in both sources, Gnostic and canon.

Jesus tells the disciples, "Become full" (3:35–38), and "then Peter replied, 'Lo, three times you have told us, "Become [full] but] we are full"'" (3:39–4:1). This corresponds to Jesus "coming a third time" in Mark 14:41 and Matthew 26:44, meaning in their meditation, of course. Peter "denies" him *three times in all four canonicals.* This denial may even be paired to "[woe] to those who have not spoken to him" in the Apocryphon of James 3:20 because it is *Peter* who asks the beloved disciple to ask Jesus who is the betrayer. (James is the one he asks, but more on that later.) At 4:5 Jesus says that "it is good to be full, and bad to be in want" and that "they who are in want will not [be saved]." This confirms that it is meditation that saves, because they are told to be "filled" three times, and it is "*for this cause* [that you may not be in want] that I have said to you, 'Be full.'" Here, Jesus tells them that it is good to be both full and in want, in a Zen koen (4:5–15): "Hence just as it is good that you (sg., Peter) be in want, and conversely, bad that you be full, so he who is full is in want, and he who is in want does not become full as he who is in want becomes full, and he who has been filled, in turn attains due perfection." (Take your time. Nobody said God-realization would be easy!)

The disciples ask that they be granted not to be tempted at 4:30, the same as Jesus tells them to "watch and pray that you enter not into temptation" (Matt. 26:41 and Mark 14:38). Jesus then tells them to "cease loving the flesh" and being afraid of suffering. "Or do you not know that you have yet to be abused and to be accused unjustly…?" (5:10–15). This is very important for understanding the Gospel of Judas. Judas and the others are told at 56:7–8 in the Gospel of Judas that they will be *tormented tomorrow.* Here you have independent confirmation that it is they, and not Jesus, about whom Jesus is speaking! What follows immediately in the Gospel of Judas is "You will sacrifice the man who bears me," the same description *of them* in the "tomorrow *he who bears me* will be tormented" just before it. Jesus therefore is telling Judas in the Gospel of Judas that it is *he* who "bears him," not Jesus. "Therefore become seekers for death, like the dead who seek for life; for that which they seek is revealed to them" (6:5–10). Remember, this is the Apocryphon *of James,* protagonist. It is tracking right along with the Gospel of Judas with *Judas* as protagonist and with the canonicals, with Judas as James. "Verily I say unto you, none of those who fear death will be saved; for the kingdom <of God> [translator emendation] belongs to those who put themselves to death" (6:15–20) (they who "sacrifice the man").

"The Lord answered and said, 'Do you not know that the head of prophecy was cut off with John?' But I [James] said, 'Lord can it be possible to remove the head of prophecy?' The Lord said to me, 'When you [pl.] come to know what "head" means, and that prophecy issues from the head, [then] understand the meaning of "its head was removed." At first I spoke to you in parables and you did not understand; now I speak to you openly, and you [still] do not perceive. Yet it was you who served me in a parable in parables, and as that which is open in the [words] that are open'" (6:25–7:10). This sounds like the heavenly redeemer telling James that he is the one, or among the ones, to succeed John the Baptist: "Yet it was you who served me ... in the *words that are open* [pl.]." "Open" will probably have a deeper meaning upon closer examination, referring to the Word of salvation.

"'Do not allow the kingdom of heaven to wither; for it is like a palm shoot whose fruit has dropped down around it. They, [the fallen fruit] put forth leaves, and after they have sprouted, they caused their wombs to dry up. So it is also with the fruit which had grown from this single root; when it had been picked [?], fruit had been borne by many'"[?].This is the disciples of Jesus. "It [the root] was certainly good, [and] if it were possible for you to produce the new plants now, < you > [sg.] would find it [the new "plants," or the disciples of the new Master]" (7:22–35). Here is Jesus telling James that he will be a savior of others.

"Since I have already been glorified in this fashion, why do you [pl.] hold me back in my eagerness to go?" (7:35–38). Jesus has done his work: "For after the [labor], you have compelled me to stay with you another eighteen days for the sake of the parables." He is done cultivating his crop of initiates, but they say they still need him to teach them.

Jesus then berates them for making him stay around "another eighteen days for the sake of the parables" that some of them understood, but not all, apparently. He then lists eight of the Synoptic parables by name: 8:1–10.

Jesus tells them to "be clear minded [Robinson's NHC translator Francis Williams has here "be sober"]; do not be deceived. And many times have I said to you all together, and also to you alone, James, have I said, 'Be saved!', and I have commanded you [sg.] *to follow me* [italics added], and I have taught you what to say to the archons" [further elucidated in First Apocalypse of James] (8:25–35). The "follow me" dynamic comes up in several other spots in the "betrayal," like the naked young man, for example, and with Peter in the courtyard.

"Therefore, trust in me, my brethren; understand what the great light is. The father has no need of me—for the father does not need a son, but it is the son that needs the father—though I go to Him. For the Father of the son *has no need of you*" [italics added] (9:10–20). Here is "sacrifice the man" again.

"Harken to the Word [the Apophasis Logos]; understand knowledge; love life, and no one will persecute you, nor will anyone oppress you, other than you yourselves" [wrath against self] (9:15–20). The disciples are told that the inner Master will protect them, as he does in the Gospel of Judas at 56:7–8. "Now therefore, follow me *quickly*" [italics added] (10:25) parallels Judas being told, "What you are going to do, do quickly" in John 13:27. The command is to "follow me" as Master, and he means now, or "quickly," "immediately." "This is why I say unto you, 'For your sakes I came down.' You are the beloved; you are they who will be the cause of life in many'" (10:29–32). It's pretty clear here that the disciples are to succeed Jesus as saviors. The Apocryphon of James informs John 13 as a remake of a Mastership installation event, not a betrayal.

"Verily I say unto you, woe to those for whose sake I was sent down to this place ... become like those who are not, that you may be with those who are not" (13:10–15). It is clear by now that the disciples are to cease to exist, individually. "Sacrifice the man who bears me" will be everywhere in these texts.

After a beautiful section on how Jesus gave faith to them, sometimes urging them on and sometimes "turning us back," a dynamic not unknown in Eastern mysticism, he then tells them that even if the Father "wishes to banish him," the disciple "who will receive life and believe in the kingdom will never leave it," something also found in Eastern teaching (13:15–14:20).

At 14:35, Jesus says, "I shall strip myself, that I may clothe myself [with themselves]." This is Mark 14:51–52, and the "young man" who "follows him" is James succeeding Jesus. After leaving "the linen cloth" of the worldly life behind and "fleeing" or ascending, the disciples are "seizing him" as the successor. "But give heed; blessed are they who have proclaimed the Son before his descent, that when I have come, I may ascend [again]. Thrice blessed are they who [were] proclaimed by the Son before they came to be, that you might have a portion among them" (14:35–15:5). Blessed when marked, blessed when accepting the Son within themselves, and blessed when the Son comes.

The Apocryphon of James ends with a section on the making of Masters out of the disciples, James describing hearing the Logos as "hymns and angelic benedictions and angelic rejoicing" (15:19–20), and ascending (15:26). After telling the others what he saw upon ascending "to the Majesty," James and Peter are asked by the others, "What did you [pl.] hear from the Master? And what has he said to you? And where did he go?" (15:30). This echoes the passage in the Gospel of Judas where the disciples ask Jesus, "Teacher, where did you go and what did you do after you left us?" (36:13–15). He answers, "I went to another great and holy race" (thus proving he didn't need help leaving his body by any planned death).

James and Peter (in the Apocryphon) answer the others: "He has ascended and has given us a pledge and promised life to us all and revealed to us children who are to come after us, after bidding [us] love them, as we would be [saved] for their sakes.

"And when they heard [this], they indeed believed the revelation, but were displeased about those to be born. And so not wishing to give them offense, I sent each one to another place. But I myself went up to Jerusalem, praying that I might obtain a portion among the beloved, who will be made manifest.

"And I [James] pray that the beginning may come from you, for thus I shall be capable of salvation, since they will be enlightened through me, by my faith—and through another [faith] that is better than mine, for I would like that mine be the lesser. Endeavor earnestly, then, to make yourself like them and pray that you may obtain a portion with them. For because of what I have said, the Savior did not make the revelation to us for their sakes. We do, indeed, proclaim a portion with those for whom the proclamation was made, those whom the Lord has made his sons" (15:35–16:30).

The passage above is one of the most astounding things ever written about salvation in the age of Christ. Here is James relating the salvation of "those for whom the proclamation was made"—the souls ("children") of those saved by the ones saved by the other disciples. The Savior did not make the revelation "for their sake" ("them" with whom they are to obtain "a portion"); that is, the saved who are saved directly by the disciples, but for those "children" to come, who are saved by those whom *they* save. Three generations are thus saved here: the disciples, their disciples, and then *the disciples of those disciples*. James is, therefore, obviously instrumental in the divine plan of salvation.

Here is a chain of Mastership succession to save souls—disciples, enjoying a revelation not made for those they saved, but for those whom *their* disciples saved—"proclaiming a portion" with those for whom the proclamation was made, the third generation. ("For their sakes" may be a mistranslation in that "did not make the revelation for *our* sakes" makes more sense, in keeping with "we would be [saved] for their sakes" stated earlier.) This third generation is also found in John17:20; only there, it is sanitized of any overt admission that the disciples are *themselves* to become saviors. In the Gnostic texts, buried and protected from the church as they were, there is no such hesitancy: "For thus I [James] shall be capable of salvation." Is there any room here for Jesus to say, "No one comes to the Father, but by me" (John 14:6)? Yes, what he means, of course, is that no one comes to the Father but by him among those who have "seen him." See John 14:7, the context of 14:6.

The next two selections from the Nag Hammadi Library collection, the First Apocalypse of James and the Second Apocalypse of James, will make it clear beyond all doubt that the canonical Gospels' story of betrayal is derived fiction. These are the original tradition—the Mastership succession dynamic—not the canonical derivation. The evidence is in comparing the details, the order of the details, and the fact that no Gnostic writer would ever borrow from an orthodox composition about sacrifice, especially human sacrifice, as a *source* for material.

The First Apocalypse of James (V, 3)

Orthodox bias is evident even here, in the introduction to this tractate in *The Nag Hammadi Library* by William R. Schoedel. He says, "An oblique and very brief reference to the crucifixion in 30:12–13" is that which reads, 'The Lord said farewell to him [James] and fulfilled what was fitting.'"[25] No, that is not a reference to crucifixion. The text says nothing about Jesus crucified. Neither does the Gospel of Judas. This is Jesus telling James that the archons, inner powers of the heavenly regions, will seize him but will not succeed in detaining him. The entire story of succession told here in the First and Second Apocalypses of James was inverted in the canonical Gospel story into one of betrayal. As astounding as it may seem, we will see the story unfold line by line,

---

25   William R. Schoedel, introduction in Robinson, *The Nag Hammadi Library,* 260.

always inverted from an account of conquering archons (conquering elements of self on the inner planes) into a pedestrian story of earthly treachery. The reason was simple. It was to hide that James the Just was the real Master. The proto-orthodox of the early church wanted converts. They could not abide a true Master and his successors in their midst, telling the truth about the false teachings of sacrificial salvation. Salvation has *never* had anything to do with sacrifice of others – only self! Other competent investigators are formulating the basis for a rejection of the orthodox Christian teaching of salvation through the death of the savior. There are so many examples of misappropriated scriptural "prophecies" and mistranslations of quotes likely uttered by a true Master (probably James) that to go into them all would require a volume of its own. Many are covered in the author's first book on saviors John and James.[26] Salvation was through Gnosis. It still is. Gnosis is the Shabd—the living Word, delivered by real Masters. Modern mystic teaching is readily accessible online. Volumes cited in this work alone are sufficient to show that Gnostic teaching and modern mystic teaching are one and the same.

Researchers Dr. Richard Carrier, Dr. Robert Price, Earl Doherty, David Fitzgerald, Hyam Maccoby, and Richard Pervo place the case for Mythicism of Christ on a solid foundation (as opposed to the 'Historicism' of a human Jesus). This present work focuses on the gnostic truths that were cleverly overwritten by the betrayal story of the New Testament and show how the latter cannot be original.

This author obtained access in 2015 to a translation of First and Second Apocalypses of James as The Apocalypse of Ya'aqov (online at Yahad. com) from a now-lost source called The Anabathmoi Jacobi (The Ascents of James). In it, James is described as lecturing on the inner regions from successively higher steps of the temple. A translation by Dr. Gush Patel will be used to fill in lacunae from the Nag Hammadi versions. This version seems to be the more accurate of the two in most cases, where there are differences in the translations, based on the

---

[26]   Wahler, *The Bible Says 'Saviors' – Obadiah 1:21*, 240.

mystic reading of the text. Some differences are confirmatory, such as "wrath *against yourself*" (NHC 32:10) of one against the other in cases of disagreement between Nag Hammadi Codex (NHC) and Tchacos Codex (CT), such as this. The Tchacos Codex has no wrath "against yourself," but the other two do. Since this is a Gnostic text, and the next line is "But this is so that these others might come to be," there is no question that wrath "against yourself" is the correct translation. And this is a pivotal line in the First Apocalypse of James, since, coming as it does just before the Gospel of Judas, it informs the Judas text at a critical juncture about just who is angry at whom. Judas is seen as *turning on himself* to assume the mantle of Mastership (CT56:23). Otherwise, we are left to wonder and must figure it out from context (which is still possible). Once we examine all the other amazing connections between these two texts and the New Testament, it will be clear that the "wrath" the author speaks of is wrath upon Judas himself. Whole technical papers have been written by scholars on Gnostic anger, but there is no mention of wrath against self.

Lest anyone think it mere coincidence when going through the many connections shown, remember that the order of corresponding details also contributes to the case that one or the other of these texts – gnostic or canonical-is derivative. Dr. Robert Eisenman has shown in his exhaustive research on the Dead Sea Scrolls Pesherim (commentaries, not the biblical texts) that the *modus operandi* of the Pauline New Testament writers, Paul, authors of Matthew, Mark, Luke, John, and Acts, and the many pseudepigraphical letters, is one of reversal, or inversion, of the Jamesian Qumran community, or *Yahad*.[27] At their self-exile in Qumran in the first century were Jamesian "Jewish Christians," who practiced serious blood-purity observances (no niece marriage, no eating carrion or "things sacrificed to idols," and no sleeping with women in their time of menstruation). Some of these things were tacitly approved of by Paul and reversed in the Gospels' story of the blood sacrifice of Jesus Christ. Paul may have conceptualized only a heavenly redeemer figure

---

27   Eisenman, *James the Brother of Jesus*, 883.

in Christ Jesus, not the human Jesus, but the New Testament Gospel authors left no doubt that they thought Jesus bled real blood for us. It never happened. What follows is proof that the story was taken from the Gnostics *and reversed.*

The First Apocalypse of James (NHC book V), The Apocalypse of James (Ascents of James, or A.J.), or James (CT)

"It is the Lord who spoke with me: 'See now the completion of my redemption. I have given you a sign of these things, James, my brother. For not without reason have I called you my brother, although you are not my brother materially. *You are* [A.J.] ignorant concerning yourself, so that when I give you a sign—know and hear'" (24:1–15). In Mark 14:44 and Matthew 26:48 we find, "Now the betrayer had *given them a sign,* saying, 'The one I shall kiss is the man; seize him and lead him away safely.'" (All italics added to scripture are for clarity, except when the source is other than NHC.) What was the "sign" originally? "I shall, however, reveal to you what has come forth from him who has no number. I shall give a sign concerning their number. As for what has come forth from him who has no measure, I shall give a sign concerning their 'measure'" (26:8–13). "See now the completion of my redemption. I have given you a sign of these things, my brother." The New Testament says this "sign" is the "kiss" of betrayal. What do the Gnostics say?

Paul stating that James was the "Lord's brother" in Galatians 1:19 may or may not have been a later interpolation to counter this very assertion in the First Apocalypse of James that Jesus and James were not brothers, but the fact that "Hail, brother!" (2 James 50:10) was changed to "Hail, Master!" (Matt. 26:49) in the canonicals' kiss scene is probably not accidental, given the later orthodox interest in the virgin birth.

"Nothing existed except Him-who-is. He is unnamable and ineffable. I myself am also unnamable, from Him-who-is…" (24:20).Both "unnamable" and "ineffable" are in the Gospel of Judas, as the realm "never called by any name" (47:13) and "Apophasis [Logos]," incipit, respectively. "Apophasis," again, means "that which is said without saying," in other words, unspoken or ineffable. "For they will seize me the day after tomorrow. But my redemption will be near" (25:5–10). Codex Tchacos, Meyer et al, has "deliverance" (Greek "paradidomi," or "delivered," becoming "betrayed" in Matthew 26:21, 23, and 46). "But leave Jerusalem. For it is she who always gives the cup of bitterness to the sons of light" (25:15). Compare this to Matthew 26:39: "Let this *cup* pass from me." "She [Jerusalem] is a dwelling place of a great number of archons [rulers of inner regions]. Yet your redemption will be preserved from them. But remember—they are but twelve powerful archons. They are not all- powerful *or even faithful to their own"* (A.J.for25:20–30). Well, well. We have unfaithful archons, *twelve* of them. Does this begin to sound familiar?

"I shall give a sign concerning their number. As for what has come forth from him, who has no measure, I shall give a sign concerning their number" (26:10). James replies that he has "received their number," and it is "seventy-two heavens" (twelve regions of heaven times the six chakras of the Adamic makeup of man), the seventy-two realms or aeons of the Gospel of Judas (50:17). "The inferior power among them [Saklasor Yaldabaoth] [brought forth] for itself angels [and] unnumbered hosts" (25:25). This "host" apparently gets inverted in Matthew 26:53 and the "twelve legions of angels" that Christ can call up to help him out after the arresting party and disciples draw swords in the Garden. "If you want to give them [these hosts] a number, you [will] not be able to do so until you *cast away* from yourself blind thought, this bond of flesh which encircles you. And then you will reach Him-who-is. *And you will no longer be James*; rather you are the One-who-is" (27:1–10). "Castaway" is a Qumranism for unrighteousness.[28] Here it is probably traceable to Luke 22:41, where Jesus "withdrew from them about a stone's *throw*, and knelt down and prayed."

Here, too, of course, is the first reference to the "sacrifice of the

---

28   DeConick, *The Codex Judas Papers*, note 144, 279. (Matt. 26:49).

man," *James* (Judas) who "bears" the Master, Jesus. But what is most important in this first scene is the "sign." 26:10–11: "I shall give a sign concerning their number. If you want to give them a number you will not able to do so until you cast away from yourself blind thought, this bond of flesh that encircles you." So, how is it that James is to "cast away" this "bond of flesh" that entraps him—the "sign"? Follow the trail.

"<James said, 'Then, > Rabbi, in what way shall I reach Him-who-is, since all these powers and hosts are armed against me?' He said to me, 'These powers are not armed against you specifically, but against another. They arm against me! They are armed against other powers. But they are armed against me in judgment. They did not give me that which was due me or go through me, so it is for me to go through them. In their place of torment and wretched agony, I will endure. The El Elyon [Eleleth in the Gospel of Judas] will stand with me, and though I could rebuke in His name, I will not. There will be a silence and a hidden mystery within me. Yet I am faint before their anger'" [A.J. for] (27:10–28:5). Could this be the origin of the vivid "bloody sweat"—the "agony" of Jesus praying apart from the others in "silence" with the angel appearing to strengthen him as a "hidden mystery"? (Luke 22:41–45). Perhaps so, perhaps not. The trail of emancipation for James continues.

"James said, 'Rabbi, if they arm themselves against you, then [there is no blaming you for taking up the sword of your mouth against them]'" [A.J.for] (28:5). Note the sword wielding by Peter (in John) and the (right) ear-cutting incident of Malchus in all Gospels. More on this later.

"The Lord said, 'James, I praise your understanding, and [respect your enduring fear]. If you continue to be distressed, be concerned for nothing else but your own [deliverance]. For behold, I shall complete this destiny upon this earth as I have said from the heavens. And I shall reveal to you your [deliverance]" (CT 15:19–22 for 29:5–10).

"James said, 'Rabbi, how after these things, will you appear to us again? After they seize you, and you complete this destiny, you will go up to Him-who-is.' The Lord said, 'James, after these things I shall reveal to you everything, not for your sake alone, but for the sake of [the] unbelief of men, so that *[faith] may exist in them* [for a vast multitude will come to faith and they will increase in days, works, and knowledge]" [A.J. for] (29:10–25). Note, "Simon, Simon, behold, Satan demanded to have you [pl.],that he might sift you [pl.] like wheat, but I have prayed for you that your *faith may not fail;* and when you have turned again, strengthen your brethren" (Luke 22:31–32). We are still waiting to see what the sign is.

"'And for this reason I shall [appear] in order to rebuke the rulers, [and I shall] reveal to them that there is one who cannot be grasped. When he is grasped, then he becomes strong. So now I shall go. Remember what I have said, and let it grow within you.' [James speaks:] 'I shall make every effort, Rabbi, to do as you have said'. And Jesus left and prepared what was destined for him" (CT 15:16–27) for 30:1–10). This is a very deep mystical passage. The real Master is within, as the Shabd, or Logos. "So now I shall go" is Jesus leaving physically, so James must focus on the inner Master, the Logos. He is the one who "cannot be grasped." "Remember what I have said" is about the Logos given to James. James is to let it grow within himself, as is his destiny. Jesus left and prepared what was destined *"for him"*—that is, *for James.* Compare this with John 13:33: "Little children, yet a little while I am with you. You will seek me; and as I said to the Jews, so now I say to you, 'Where I am going you cannot come." The Son of man will be glorified *in James* (John 13:31–32), not in Jesus.

"When James heard of his sufferings and was much distressed, they awaited the sign of his coming. And he came after several days. James [was walking up the hill called Golgotha [Gaugelam, NHC, CT] with his disciples who listened closely to him, for they had been greatly distressed. James became the Paraclete ["Comforter," NHC, CT—the Master] for them all, saying, 'This is the hill of death upon which the Just One [Jesus] came to life a second time'" or, as the CT version has this line, "And they had him as a Comforter, saying 'This is the second master.'" The disciples left that place, and James remained behind, "praying long hours as was his custom" [CT and A.J. for] (30:10–31:1). Either way this is read, the disciples recognized James as the new Master and themselves as "*his* disciples." DeConick mentions this reference to the "twelve disciples" of James.[29] Several parallels to the canon are evident here: James praying on Gaugelan (compare, Golgotha), and Jesus praying on the Mount of Olives (Luke 22:39, Gethsemane in Mark and Matthew); "walking on"/"went out to" the hill/the mountain; the group of disciples leaving James alone to pray, and Jesus "[withdrawing] from them about a stone's throw and [kneeling] down and [praying]" (Luke 22:41); "distress," "sorrow," and "death/hill of death" in Matthew 26:37–38 and Mark 14:33–34, with Luke's agony of the bloody sweat all following the arrival of James/Jesus to pray. And Jesus still has not fulfilled the sign of his coming.

"And the Lord appeared to him" (31:2). This pairs in time and place to "and he came ..." (Mark 14:37, 40, and 41; Matt. 26:40, 42, and 43; and Luke 22:45). We will see this dynamic of coming in the Gnostic Apocalypse of Peter in a stunning revelation of what "coming" means here.

"Then James ceased his praying and embraced the Master. He kissed him, saying, 'Rabbi, I have found you! I have heard of your sufferings, which you have endured, and I have been much distressed. My compassion you know. Therefore, on reflection, I was wishing I would not see this people. They must be judged for these things that they have done. For these things that they have done are contrary to what is fitting'" (31:3–14). This sounds like a good description of a hoard of soldiers coming with Judas to arrest Jesus: Mark 14:43, Matthew 26:47, Luke 22:47, John 18:3. Compare this to "It is enough!" ("ceased his praying"); "And he kissed him" (Matt. 26:49; Mark 14:41,45; Luke 22:47); and "Hail, Master!" "The Master said, 'James, do not be concerned for me or for these people. I am He who was within me. Never have I suffered in anyway, nor have I been distressed. These people have done me no harm. They have come here as a type of archons, and what was destroyed here deserved to be destroyed by them. Now that the archons have been deceived by the destructive actions of these people, and since I am free

---

29   DeConick, The Codex Judas Papers, note 144, 279. (Matt. 26:49).

of the imposter, the archons are now maliciously angry with you, my brother, because you are now the pillar upon which the world balances. Now, your name will be James the Just One'" [A.J. for] (31:14–32:3). The "things that they have done contrary to what is fitting" are the archons mistreating Jesus in the heavens in the Apocalypse version, not the arrest party abusing Jesus here on earth in the canon. "Never have I suffered in any way" and "these people have done me no harm" are paralleled in the Gospel of Judas at 56:9–11: "No hand of a mortal human will sin against me." Note that James says, "I have been distressed," not that Jesus is distressed.

All this is in the right time and place to correspond to the narrative in the Gnostic Apocalypse of First James. The spiritual "kiss" between James and Jesus is the sign. It is, of course, inverted tendentiously to become a kiss of betrayal between Judas and Jesus. This is the Shabd, or Word, the "sword of his mouth," not the sign of his betrayal. In the canonical narrative, "Judas" is always James inverted, but sometimes the character Jesus even parallels James. This does make the story somewhat hard to follow, but it is the only way to make sense of it all. Dr. Eisenman has other characters covering James, such as Stephen, John Mark, Nathaniel, and James Zebedee. Lazarus, the "beloved disciple," and other unnamed characters ("a young man" in Mark 14:51, "one of them" in the Synoptics betrayal, and "the other disciple" in John 18:15–16) may all also be stand-ins for James. The idea was, after all, to hide James, a well-known public figure of his time, known to historians.

The foot-washing episode in John 13:12–20 is the Johannine equivalent to this "I am" section of First Apocalypse of James. In it, Judas is supposedly indicated as the betrayer, but he is not—at least not in the original quotations of the Master, Jesus: "Do you know what I have done to you? You call me Teacher and Lord; and you are right, for so I am. If I then, your Lord and teacher, have washed your feet, you also ought to wash one another's feet. For I have given you an example, that you also should do as I have done to you. Truly, truly, I say to you, a servant is not greater than his Master; *nor is he who is sent greater than he who sent him.* If you know these things, blessed are you if you do them. I am not speaking of you all. *I know whom I have chosen;* it is that the scripture be fulfilled, 'He who ate my bread has lifted his heel against me.' I tell you this now, before it takes place, that when it does take place you may believe *that I am he.* Truly, truly, I say to you, he who receives anyone whom I send receives me; and he who receives me receives Him who sent me." Jesus desires that the disciples learn to accept *his successor.* All these verses are about succession, not about betrayal. He says, "I know whom *I have chosen.*" He would not be changing subjects from "nor is he who is sent greater than he who sent him" to the betrayer—and then back to "I am he" and "any one whom I send receives me." The scriptural referent at 13:18 (Psalm41:9) must be a positive, or at least neutral, statement about his emissary, or successor. And, as it turns out, it is. This will be covered in a later section on mistranslation of key verses in the "betrayal."

"See, already you have been released, since you will know me and you will know yourself, and you yourself even stopped this prayer that the Just God [Yaldabaoth, Satan] prayed. Now that you are the Just One, the Man of Elohim, you recognize me so as to embrace and kiss me. Amen! I say to you that you have stirred up great anger and wrath *against yourself.* Yet you were not afraid and you kissed me. This has happened so that all these others might also come to be" [A.J. for] (32:3–12), meaning that the "wrath" is for the good of others—a good thing, not a bad thing. The kiss is the moment of realization, the "sign," when James receives gnosis from Jesus, the "sacrifice [of] the man who bears me" (56:20–21). Since it isn't part of the Gospel of Thomas, the Gospel of Judas tradition may well be the most primitive telling of the transfer of Mastership even among the Gnostic texts: "The Unspoken Word in which Jesus *spoke* with Judas Iscariot" (Gospel of Judas incipit). The "sword of his mouth" from this Apocalypse of James was still merely an "unspoken" Word in the Gospel of Judas, not yet a "kiss." Following it in the Gospel of Judas is the ode to the new "Param Sant" initiating Master, with his "horn raised," his "wrath stirred up" *against self,* his "star ascended," and his "heart grown strong" This for the task ahead, for Judas to lead "all these others," those who "might also come to be" saved. Again, without these parallels in the First Apocalypse of James, we would not know with whom Judas was angry. His "heart has grown strong" perhaps is a distant foreshadowing of the kiss that was not yet a part of the Mastership installation tradition. After all, it isn't in the received portions of the Gospel of Judas! Unfortunately, the canon inverted this beautiful sign of the coming of James—a coming so that "all these others might come to be." If not for the serendipity of finding these amazing apocryphal texts, we might never have known what the "betrayal of Jesus" was really all about. Be sure to thank the nameless monks in your prayers who had the inspiration of hiding the Apocalypses of James and the Gospel of Judas from their oppressors.

"But James was timid [and] wept. And he was very distressed. And they both sat down upon a rock. Jesus said to him, 'James, thus you will undergo these sufferings. But do not be sad, for the flesh is weak. It will receive what has been ordained for it. But as for you, do not be [timid] or afraid.' The Lord [ceased]" (32:13–23). "The Lord *ceased*" is even in order with Matthew's "Thy will *be done*" (26:42). "The flesh is weak" is a key phrase in Mark and Matthew for showing the close affinity of the Gnostic texts with the canonical Gospels, and it comes intertwined in the narrative with "sorrow" (Matthew and Mark), "suffering" (Luke's "agony"), and "sitting" with Peter and the Zebedee brothers (including James), in Matthew. This passage of the distress James felt alone should convince anyone that this is original. The kiss is James receiving the assignment of Master, and it is he that is distressed, not Jesus. The theme of sorrow and distress amplifies in Luke's description of the agony and bloody sweat chiasmus climax (which is a proven interpolation because it interrupts the poetic structure of the chiasmus in Luke 22:39-46). The only suffering that Jesus experienced in the original narrative was at the hands of the archons, which James felt in his distress (30:15). James is the one experiencing all the distress, and he will suffer, not Jesus, even though in the Apocalypse he has suffered *already* under the attacks of the spiritual archons. There is a persistent transference of what James *has already experienced* in the

Gnostic accounting to what Jesus *will be experiencing* in the canon. How can the story's origin be reversed to the canon as original? There is no record outside the canon for any of the arrest, trial, and death of Jesus. There is for James—*and for all three!*

The next segment, First James 32:23–33:28, is paralleled in the arrest scene of John 18: "The Lord said to him, 'James, behold, I shall reveal to you your redemption [deliverance, CT]. When you are seized, and you undergo these sufferings, *a multitude will arm themselves against you* that< they > may seize you. And in particular, three of them will seize you—they who sit [there] as toll collectors. Not only do they demand tolls, *but they take away souls by theft.* When you come into their power, one of them who is their guard will say to you, "Who are you?"'" This is spoken twice, to which Jesus replies, "I am a son" and "I am a son in the Pre-existent One," just as in John 18 he says, "I am he" and "I told you, I am he," with the soldiers and officers "withdrawing" and curiously "falling down" in good mystic meditation fashion. One has to wonder just what is going on here. The answer is in the Malchus "prophecy" of John 18:9–10, another mistranslation, taken up soon in the New Testament section.

"But when you come to [these] three detainers who take away souls by theft in that place, [you will be the vessel of authority—and much more than just a vessel. You shall be the Just One for whom the world came to be]" [A.J. for] (34:21–30). Echoing that other early Gnostic text, the Gospel of Thomas, this text now flatly points to James as the new Master and leader of the Assembly. Interestingly, John 18:12 has three detainers: "So the band of soldiers and their captain and the officers of the Jews seized Jesus and bound him." Or, if you like, Mark 14:43 has "the chief priests, the scribes, and the elders."

The stoning of James is only recounted in the Codex Tchacos version of the First Apocalypse of James, not the Anabathmoi Jacobi or the Nag Hammadi Codex (CT 30:23). Relate this to the vision of Judas in the Gospel of Judas 44:24–27 (and also the stoning of Stephen in Acts 7, a cover story for the stoning of James, per Dr. Eisenman). The Nag

Hammadi and Anabathmoi Jacobi texts of the Second Apocalypse of James have this interesting line leading into the stoning: "And he [James] went at that time [immediately] and rebuked the twelve, and cast out of them contentment [concerning the] way of Gnosis" (42:20–24). Is this why Judas sees them stoning him ("Judas" as James) in the Gospel of Judas? The third-century author of the Pseudoclementine Recognitions 1:70 has followers of Paul attacking James.[30]

We know that there was contention or quarreling in the Luke 22:24 passage about who was the greatest among them. Perhaps this has something to do with why Judas will "exceed them all." The Tchacos Codex version has "And when they were stoning [him], he said, 'My Father, you [who are in the] heavens, forgive them for they know < not > what they are doing" (30:23–26). We obviously must reconcile this with Luke 23:24: "And Jesus said, 'Father, forgive them; for they know not what they do." Dr. Eisenman points out in his work that a similar statement is made by "Stephen" at his death by stoning in Acts 7, among other details showing that Stephen covers for James.[31]

The Second Apocalypse of James (V, 4)

The introduction to Robinson's *The Nag Hammadi Library* Second Apocalypse of James by Charles W. Hedrick begins, "The fourth tractate in Codex V has been given the modern title *The (Second) Apocalypse of James* in order to distinguish it from the preceding tractate, since both documents have the same ancient title: *The Apocalypse of James.*

"The tractate contains at least four sections artistically arranged. Because of their balance and stylized form they have been described as 'harmonic prose' possessing a 'hymnic' quality. Three of these units are aretalogies.[32] One (49.5–15) is a series of self-assertions by the resurrected Jesus in the 'I am' style. Another (58.2–20) is a series of predications about the resurrected Jesus made by James in the third

---

30   Christian Classics Ethereal Library, http://www.ccel.org/ccel/schaff/anf08.vi.iii. iii.lxx.html

31   Eisenman, *James the Brother of Jesus,* 441-443.

32   According to Wiktionary, this is "that part of moral philosophy which treats of virtue, its nature, and the means of attaining to it."

person (i.e., 'he is'). In a further aretalogy (55.15–56,13) the resurrected Jesus describes James' special role in the second person (i.e., 'you are'). The entire description in the third aretalogy suggests that James is intended to perform the function of gnostic redeemer. The fourth unit (62.16–63.29) is a prayer attributed to James.

"The tractate as a whole is clearly gnostic in character, yet it shows remarkable restraint in treating usual gnostic themes. *Nor can it be identified with any of the known gnostic systems of the second century* [italics added]. On the other hand, the author has made extensive use of Jewish- Christian traditions. James, who held a position of special prominence in Jewish-Christian circles, is regarded as the possessor of a special revelation from Jesus and is assigned a role in the gnostic tradition *that rivals, and perhaps exceeds, that of Peter* in the canonical tradition. For example, James is the 'escort' who guides the Gnostic through the door of the heavenly kingdom and even rewards him (55:6–14;cf.55:15–56.3). The description is similar to Peter's charge as the keeper of the keys of heaven (Mt.16:19).

"As to the date and place of composition, little can be said with certainty. Because of the basic Jewish-Christian traditions out of which the tractate is composed, it is probable that its origin is to be associated with Jewish-Christian circles. *The absence of allusions to the later developed gnostic systems, and the almost total absence of allusions to the New Testament tradition suggest an early date for the tractate* [italics added]."[33] This is, therefore, *an early work* in the Christian tradition, at least rivaling the canonical Gospels.

Starting on the "fifth flight of steps, the highly esteemed place," James is a Master. The fifth region is the Imperishable Region of Sant Mat—*Sach Khand*.[34] "James spoke, 'You all know me. I am he who received revelation from the Pleroma [of] Imperishability'" (46.5-8).

With nearly a dozen "I am" statements in the first section (46-49),the Gnostics were the first to use this form, not the author of John: "I am he who received revelation from the Pleroma [of] Imperishability. [I am] he who was first summoned by him who is great, and who

---

[33]   Charles W. Hedrick, introduction for Robinson, *The Nag Hammadi Library,* 269-270.

[34]   Swami Ji, *Sar Bachan,* 28-35.

obeyed the [Lord]—he who passed through [the heavens, A.J.] into the [world]; he who stripped himself and went about naked, he who was found in a perishable [state], though he was about to be brought up to Imperishability" (46:6–19). There is a parallel here to Mark 14:52–52: "And a young man followed him, with nothing but a linen cloth about his body; and they seized him, but he left the linen cloth and [fled] naked." The Greek word in Mark 14 is "pheugo," which can mean "went about" and not "ran away," like the English NIV and RSV have. The King James version has "fled," as do most other early versions. There is obvious confusion among the Christian scribes as to what to make of this enigmatic passage. Now we know. The fact that this was originally one of the "I am" statements as seen in the Second Apocalypse of James means that the Markan "stripped and fleeing naked" passage as well as the "I am" Johannine formulation were both original to the Gnostics. The next line from the Gnostic account shows that the "young man" was James, and that "stripping naked" has to do with becoming a Master: "This *Present Master* came as a son who seeks and as a brother was he sought" [A.J.for] (46:20–23). This is possibly the source of the Pauline "James, the brother of the Lord" in Galatians 1:19. The line after that one is also on point: "He will return to the One who 'begot' him, for in him he is united and freed [stripped!], even as he came forth to unite those who found him" [A.J.for] (46:23–47:6). Much of this passage was lost in the Nag Hammadi codex version, so this gnostic reading for the Markan "young man" was news even to the present author! Other Gnostic texts exhibit "stripped and rising naked," as in the Gospel of Philip 56:26–30, and "strip off what is corrupted" in order to "become illuminators [within] mortal men" (Letter of Peter to Philip, NHC 137:6–9). Remember, the Markan version has the telltale "young man *followed* him," which is a dynamic that will reappear in the canonical examination following this section (no pun intended).

"Such things I see have already been proclaimed through these sayings: that he will be judged with *the unjust,* and he who lived without blasphemy dies by blasphemy" [A.J.for] (47:20–26). "For I tell you that the scripture must be fulfilled in me, 'And he was reckoned *with transgressors;* for what is written about me has its fulfilment" (Luke 22:37). "He who is *cast out* of temporal life *is cast* into life that is imperishable" [A.J. for] (47:27–30) becomes "And he withdrew from them about *a stone's throw,* and knelt down and prayed" (Luke 22:41). Here are two more undeniable matches of phrasing, in order and in place, in each source: gnostic Second James and the canonical Luke.

"I am the first begotten son who will destroy the dominion of them all" (49:6–9). Note that James is not the "only begotten" son any more than Jesus was the only begotten son! The "begotten" son is the Holy Spirit, that spirit which God "gave," past tense, in John 3:16, *before* he was supposedly given in death by orthodox reckoning.

"Behold, I speak in order that I may *come forth. Pay attention* to me so that you might see me!"(49:16–19). "Paying attention" means meditating. He "speaks" the Shabd, or Word. It "comes forth" in the initiate's meditation, for he who is "watching" or "rising" to the "Deliverer" within, so as to avoid temptation (Matt. 26:40–41, Mark 14:38).

"Once when I was sitting, deliberating ["meditating", A.J.], he opened the door. That one whom you hated and persecuted came into [within]me. He said to me, 'Hail, my brother; my brother, hail!' As I lifted up my eyes to stare [gaze] at him [my] mother said to me, 'Do not be frightened, my son, because he said "My brother" to you [sg.]. For you [pl.] were nourished with this same milk [the Word]. Because of this he calls me "My mother [Sophia]."For he is not a stranger to us. He is your [brother, A.J.]'" (50:1– 25). Matthew 26:49 has "Hail, Master!" at just this juncture, showing another match, in order and in place in a different Gospel paralleling the Gnostic Second Apocalypse of James. Only this time, the subject, James the "brother," is replaced by James "the Master"! This isn't Jesus who is the Master being hailed— this is James the Just hailed! Even *Jesus* is covering James. By the way, the penalty in first-century Palestine for blasphemy was stoning, not crucifixion! Now whose death fits this picture? James was tried and convicted in 62 CE, according to Josephus, for blasphemy in an illegal

Sanhedrin trial.[35] Does that not also fit? This switch to "Hail, Master!" from "Hail, my brother, my brother, Hail!" is a telling one. Why not leave it alone? At the time of the composition of the Gnostic text, one didn't have the virgin birth fiction to take into account. Later, however, when the canonical Gospels were composed, one did. The proto-orthodoxy was keen on Jesus being at least equal to the dying and rising godmen myths of the pagans. Therefore, they were increasingly intent on giving Jesus a virgin mother. Alternatively, like Dr. Eisenman says, James contributed to this aspect of the canon through his Nazirite background of lifelong celibacy. Maybe it was both. Either way, this is a clear indication of the primacy of the Gnostic tradition!

Next in Luke is the bloody sweat followed by the kiss and then the cutting of Malchus's ear. All three have troubling implications for the orthodox reading of the Gospels. Dr. Bart Ehrman shows that the bloody sweat is scribal interpolation;[36] the "kiss," we have seen is inverted from the Gnostic story of James's Mastership; and no one's ear was "cut off"—that is symbolism for initiation (of Malchus). What follows in all four canonical Gospels after the kiss is the recognition and arrest of Jesus. This is a lengthy excerpt but necessary for context:

Then he told me these words,

"I have a great many other lost brothers. But I will find them all and they will come forth. Yet I am the stranger [The Stranger, "Allogenes," CT Gnostic book four], and they have no knowledge or thought of me, for they know me only in the flesh. But it was fitting *that others might come to know me through you* [italics added].

"You are the one to whom I say: Hear and understand—for the multitude [the third time this word is used], when they hear, will be slow witted. But you [on the other hand] will be able to understand as well as I am able to explain to you.

35 Eusebius, *History of the Church*, trans. G.A. Williamson (Penguin, New York, 1989), 61.

36 Bart Ehrman, *The Orthodox Corruption of Scripture*, (Oxford: Oxford University Press, 1963), 187-189.

"Your father is not my father. But my father has become a father to you.

"This virgin about whom you hear—namely, the virgin[…]

"For this father's words [the Word] have been profitable for me, for I have listened to him; and what I tell you will likewise be profitable to you. Your father, whom you see as being rich, will grant that you inherit all these that you see! So profitable will be these words [Word] that I proclaim to you that you simply must open your ears to hear and understand [Gnosis]; then walk accordingly! It is on account of you that they pass by [ascend], made active by the Radiant One [*Sat Purush*]. Others will covet this glorious inheritance and, if they want, will cause a disturbance in order to seize possession [armed multitudes seizing, again]. For this knowledge is coveted by an inferior creator and the civilization he began yet did not finish. It is not even for those who are descending [seeJohn1:53], sent forth by him to create this present appearance of reality.

"Yet after this is made known, when the inferior creator is shamed, he shall be disturbed that his labor, which is far off from the aeons is, in fact, nothing. And his inheritance, which he boasts to be great, will in actuality be small. His gifts are not blessings. His promises are but evil schemes. For you are not an instrument of his compassion, but it is through you that he does violence. He wants to do unjustly to us all, and he will continue to exercise dominion for the time allowed him.

"But understand and know the Father who is compassionate. He has not bestowed [upon the Son] an inheritance that is limited, nor does the son have a limited number of days, but it is as eternal day for Him. We cannot say that the son has come from the fallen ones just because he is despised. Instead, he boasts in derision so that they cannot contradict him. This makes him superior to those below, those who you look down upon. After he imprisoned those belonging to the Father, he seized them and molded them to resemble himself. And it is with him that they now exist.

"I saw from the heights what events came to pass, and I have explained how they came to pass. These fallen [archons] were acquainted with me when they were in another form, and while I was watching them, they came to know me as I am, through those whom I know. Now before certain other events come to pass they will attempt to make a covenant against you, to make an end of you.

"I know how they attempted to descend upon this place so that he might approach the little children [seekers], yet I want to reveal myself through you, even the Spirit of Power, so that the Father might reveal which of these little children belong to you.

"Those who seek to walk in the way that is before the Gate and wish to enter may open the good Gate through you. And as they follow you they may enter and you may escort them inside and give a reward to each one who is ready for it" [A.J. for] (51:1–55:15).

In the above excerpt, Jesus tells James that it is through him that others will come to know him, to be saved. (See also "other sheep not of this fold" [John 10:16] and "those who believe in me through their Word" [John17:20]). The "slow-witted multitude" becomes the troop that Judas brings with him to the arrest scene, asking for Jesus twice, as if they have no clue which one he is. This comes conveniently just after the High Priestly Prayer (John17), where he outlines the salvation plan for those coming to him through James (in the passage above). James, then, is the source of the "virgin birth." He has taken a vow of chastity as a

Nazirite (Epiphanius via Eusebius). This morphs into Jesus of the virgin birth and the "young maiden"/virgin nonsense of Isaiah 7:14 ("almah"). It was *James*—not Jesus—who had virginity in his makeup. After the new initiates "*ascend,* made active by the Radiant One,"[37] we find the canonical "disturbance" and "seizing possession"—general mayhem at The Betrayal arrest of Jesus, in order and in step with this text:

> For though you are not the redeemer;
> neither a helper of strangers;
> But you are an illuminator and redeemer of those who are
> mine, and now, of those who are yours.
> You will reveal me to them;
> you will bring good to them all.
>
> You they will admire because of every powerful good work.
> You are the one whom the heavens bless.
> You [Saklas, Satan] he shall envy, he who calls himself your
> superior.
>
> I am the Gate of entrance for the ones you instructed in
> these ways.
> For your sake, they will be told all and will come to repose.
> For your sake, they will reign and will become kings.
> For your sake they will have pity on whomever they pity.
> For just as you are first having clothed yourself,
> you are also the first who will strip himself (of flesh),
> and you shall become as you were before you were stripped'
> (55:16–56:13).
>
> Then he kissed my mouth [spiritually, not physically]. He
> took hold of me saying, "My beloved one! Look! I will show
> you things that neither the heavens nor the archons have ever

---

[37] Language that could be right out of *Sar Bachan*, with the radiant form of the inner Master several other Gnostic texts, including the Gospel of Judas 56-24, also have this word form, which is not "pass by" but "ascend".

known" (Gospel of Judas, 47:2–8).

Look! I will show you things that he did not know, he who boasted that "there is no other except me." Am I not alive? Because I am a father, do I not have power to do anything? See! I will show you everything my beloved. See and know that I reveal so that you may come forth just as I AM. Look! I will even show you the Hidden One. Now stretch out your hand! Take hold of me! (56:14–57:11).

"Becoming kings" is matched in the Gospel of Judas 53:24, with Gabriel giving spirits and souls to "the kingless race." And again, there is Mark 14:51–52 and "stripped" and "becoming as you were before you were stripped."

So I stretched out my hand and I did not find him as I thought (Gospel of Judas 33:19–21). Then I heard him saying, "See me! Take hold of me!"
Then I understood, and I was afraid. And I was exceedingly joyful!

So now I tell you judges: you have been judged. You did not spare but you have been spared. Be sober [clear] and hear what you cared not to learn (57:12–58:1).

He was that One. He created the heaven and earth.
and dwelled in it, but you did not see Him.
He was the One. He is the Life.

He is the Light.
He is the one who will come.
He will provide an ending for what has begun
and a beginning for what is about to end.
He is the Ruach haKodesh—the Invisible One.

He did not fall upon the earth.
He is the virgin. He controls what he wants to happen to him.
I saw He was naked, and there were no clothes on Him.
But that is what He wills, and what He wills comes to be.
(58:2–58:25).

The final lines of the Second Apocalypse of James have a prayer by James as he is being stoned, which says in part:

Save me from an evil death!
Bring me from a tomb alive. (63:6–7).

This certainly looks like a possible source for the empty tomb passages in the canonical Gospels. More research is called for to make such a connection a firm one, however.

Second-century church father Hegesippus writes two famous quotes of Christ as original to James (via Eusebius, as the original is now lost).One is at the end of Matthew 26:64 and the other at the end of Luke 23:34 (and Luke paraphrased in Acts 7:60, the stoning of Stephen). The Hegesippus account seems a more likely prayer when being stoned than the long prayer in the Second Apocalypse of James (which is 28 lines in all):

The aforesaid scribes and Pharisees accordingly set James on the summit of the temple, and cried aloud to him, and said: "O just one, whom we are all bound to obey, forasmuch as the people is in error, and follows Jesus the crucified, do thou tell us what is the door of Jesus, the crucified." And he answered with a loud voice: "Why ask ye me concerning Jesus the Son of man? He Himself sitteth in heaven, at the right hand of the Great Power, and shall come on the clouds of heaven."

And, when many were fully convinced by these words, and offered praise for the testimony of James, and said, "Hosanna to the son of David," then again the said Pharisees and scribes said to one another, "We have not done well in procuring this testimony to Jesus. But let us go up and throw him down, that they may be afraid, and not believe him." And they cried aloud, and said: "Oh! oh! the just man himself is in error." Thus they fulfilled the Scripture written in Isaiah: "Let us away with the just man, because he is troublesome to us: therefore shall they eat the fruit of their doings." So they went up and threw down the just man, and said to one another: "Let us stone James the Just." And they began to stone him: for he was not killed by the fall; but he turned, and kneeled down, and said: "I beseech Thee, Lord God our Father, forgive them; for they know not what they do."[38]

Other Texts from Nag Hammadi:

The Gnostic (or "Coptic") Apocalypse of Peter (NHC VII, 3)

The Gnostic Apocalypse of Peter (not to be confused with the "Apocalypse of Peter" discovered during excavations directed by Sylvain Grébaut in 1886–87 in a desert necropolis at Akhmim in Upper Egypt) is a special case in this investigation. This Nag Hammadi text likely does not have the early provenance of the Apocalypses of James, given that it lacks detail showing close affinity to the canonical betrayal narrative. But there is one short phrase following a complexly worded initial passage that describes the close relationship of Master and disciple which must be considered in our examination of how the Gnostics may have influenced the canon. Translation by James Brashler and Roger A. Bullard:

As the Savior was sitting in the temple in the three hundredth

---

[38]   Eusebius, *History of the Church*, 60.

[year] of the covenant and the agreement of the tenth
pillar, and being satisfied with the number of the living,
incorruptible Majesty, he said to me, "Peter, blessed are those
above belonging to the Father, who revealed life to those who
are from the life, through me, since I reminded [them], they
who are built on what is strong, that they may hear my word,
and distinguish words of unrighteousness and transgression
of law from righteousness, as being from the height of every
word of this Pleroma of truth, having been enlightened in
good pleasure by him whom the principalities sought. But
they did not find him, nor was he mentioned among any
generation of the prophets. He has now appeared among
these, in him who appeared, who is the Son of Man, who is
exalted above the heavens in a fear of men of like essence.
But you yourself, Peter, become perfect in accordance with
your name with myself, the one who chose you, because
from you I have established a base for the remnant whom
I have summoned to knowledge. Therefore be strong
until the imitation of righteousness—of him who had
summoned you, having summoned you to know him in
a way which is worth doing because of the rejection which
happened to him, and the sinews of his hands and his feet,
and the crowning by those of the middle region, and the
body of his radiance which they bring in hope of service
because of a reward of honor—as he was about to reprove
you three times in this night."[39]

This excerpt ends with a real shock: "As he was about to reprove you three
times in this night" is remarkably similar to a reversal of Jesus famously
saying to Peter, "Truly, I tell you, this very night, before the rooster crows,
you will deny me three times" (Matt. 26:34, Mark 14:30, ESV). Here,
of course, it is Jesus denying Peter three times, and "in this night." *Three*
details paralleled in one sentence? One has to inquire: Who is borrowing

[39]   James Brashler, and Roger A. Bullard, Robinson, *The Nag Hammadi Library,* 373.

and inverting, and why? Why would the Gnostics use this strange twist of the canon to explain mystic union? Perhaps the tradition preexisted the canon? Other fabrications to show an inept and clueless Peter in the canon are not unknown (the three heavenly tablecloth visions of Acts 11, for example—as if Peter needed a revelation from heaven to tell him what to eat, for heaven's sake, *after three years* in the company of the Master! Or the thrice-repeated "Feed my sheep!" in the interpolated John 21). It seems more than likely that this third example of the repetitive three is also invention. All that can be said is that more exploration of this fascinating parallel needs to be undertaken. Note also "*the rejection which happened to him.*" That's pretty mild language for crucifixion. It sounds more like a heavenly Gnostic attack of archontic beings. Note his (later, 'thorny') "crowning," also.

What immediately follows that initial paragraph of seeing the "Radiant Form" of the Master is this beautiful poetic discussion of how one is to meditate:

> And as he was saying these things, I saw the priests and the people running up to us with stones, as if they would kill us; and I was afraid that we were going to die.

> And he said to me, "Peter, I have told you many times that they are blind ones who have no guide. If you want to know their blindness, put your hands upon [your] eyes—your robe—and say what you see."

> But when I had done it, I did not see anything. I said "No one sees [this way]."

> Again he told me, "Do it again."

> And there came in me fear with joy, for I saw a new light greater than the light of day. Then it came down upon the Savior. And I told him about those things which I saw.

> And he said to me again, "Lift up your hands and listen to what the priests and the people are saying."

And I listened to the priests as they sat with the scribes.
The multitudes were shouting with their voice.

When he heard these things from me he said to me,
"Prick up your ears and listen to the things they are saying."

And I listened again, "As you sit, they are praising you."

And when I said these things, the Savior said, "I have told
you that these [people] are blind and deaf. Now then,
listen to the things which they are telling you in a mystery,
and guard them.Do not tell them to the sons of this age.
For they shall blaspheme you in these ages since they are
ignorant of you, but they will praise you in knowledge."

The reference to "put your hands upon [your] eyes—your robe"
is misinformed. It should read, "Put your hands upon your eyes, your
covering." There must be a lot of this sort of poor word selection in the
translation process, not just here in the Coptic Apocalypse of Peter, but
in all the Nag Hammadi/Al Minya (Gospel of Judas) texts, and even in
the Greek New Testament. The author's aforementioned previous book
includes discussion of some of these more consequential mistranslations,
as does part 3 of this book. Here we see a vivid description of the process
of meditation, one which this author has experienced personally. "*As
you sit,* they are praising you [with the Sound]" is meditation. "Lift
up your hands" is not lifting up hands to cup the ears or to bow down
in "Hosanna!" fashion, but to put them, with fingers laced, over the
eyes to block out any ambient light. This allows one to ultimately see
the inner Light, that light that is "greater than the light of day." The
right thumb is placed over the right ear, so as to close it off to allow
one to listen to the Word, or Shabd, resounding endlessly within: "the
multitudes shouting with their voice… praising you." *Anyone*, with
just a little concentration, can perform this Yogic exercise and hear a
distant echo of the real "Sound Current," or Word. It is within us all.
There is even a reference to this esoteric practice in the New Testament

canon. It is the right ear 'cut off' of Malchus, discussed shortly in the next section. Many scriptural stories like the "shouting down the walls" at Jericho in Joshua 6; "calling on the Name of the Lord" in the time of Seth in Genesis 4:26; and "hearing" of the Lord that makes the ears "tingle" [or 'ring'] in 1 Samuel 3:11 are about this Word, the Apophasis Logos, or Shabd.

The next segment that wraps up this examination of the Gnostic Apocalypse of Peter is a condemnation of the Pauline proto-orthodox church, led by the antinomian, Paul—the "evil, cunning man" with "a manifold dogma" of "clinging to the name of a dead man [Jesus Christ]":

> For many will accept our teaching in the beginning. And they will turn from them again by the will of the Father of their error, because they have done what he wanted. And he will reveal them in his judgment, i.e., the servants of the Word. But those who became mingled with these shall become their prisoners, since they are without perception. And the guileless, good, pure one they push to the worker of death, and to the kingdom of those who praise Christ in a restoration. And they praise the men of the propagation of falsehood, those who will come after you. And they will cleave to the name of a dead man, thinking that they will become pure. But they will become greatly defiled and they will fall into a name of error, and into the hand of an evil, cunning man and a manifold dogma, and they will be ruled without law (73.23-74.22).

Marsanes (NHCX1), relating a key mystic initiatory detail

April DeConick mentions that "the initiate should not cease 'naming the angels'" (Nag Hammadi Codex book, Marsanes[40]) thinking that it means going on naming countless 'angels' of the inner worlds. What it really refers to is endlessly repeating a small number of important

---

[40]   DeConick, *The Codex Judas Papers*, 258.

archons' names, as a mantra for concentration—a sort of spiritual password repetition that is taught even today in mystic India.[41]

The Book of Thomas the Contender (NHC II, 7)

The gnostic book of Thomas the Contender has an undeniable reference to the withdrawal process during mystic meditation: "For they will be scourged so as to make them rush backwards, whither they do not know, and *they will recede from their limbs not patiently* but [with] despair [italics added]" (141:38). This passage describes the death of the uninitiated. The *initiated*, in contrast, experience a controlled withdrawal of consciousness from the body in their meditation.

The Gospel of the Egyptians (NHC III, 2 and IV, 2)

In the Gospel of the Egyptians, in a tractate full of lacunae that make an already difficult text nearly impossible to follow, the "Great Invisible Spirit" mentioned in the Gospel of Judas is "the silence of silent silence" [!] who brought forth, among numerous other things, the "five seals" of NHC III, 44:26–27,56:25, and 58:7, or the "Five Shabds," Swami Ji Maharaj's "Five Melodies."[42]

Pistis Sophia and the Book of Jeu

Concerning April De Conick and the problem of "daimon" and Judas as Demon of "the Thirteenth" there is Pistis Sophia and her abode in the "Thirteenth" aeon. There is no reason to assume Judas is irredeemably evil because he is said to be a "daimon." Judas leaves his lower self behind in 36:1–3, when the author of the Gospel of Judas says that his twelve elements will again "return to their God."

He is "replaced" by his Master, who is the one who ascends. "Judas" ceases to exist; he will "sacrifice the man"—himself—that bears his

---

41   Swami Ji, *Sar Bachan*, 82.

42   Swami Ji, note 16, 34.

Master, becoming one with him. Pistis Sophia also has, "I have sent Elias into John the Baptist" (135:355). This is mentioned elsewhere in this work from the Gospel of Matthew (11:11–14), and confirms reincarnation as biblical teaching.[43]

---

[43]   G.R.S. Meade, translator, gnosis.org/library/pistis-sophia/index.htm

III

The New Testament:
The Gospels as a Cover-Up of
Mastership Succession

"What I've said is that people mistake literature for history."
–Robert Eisenman, 2005, Rachel Kohn interview

There are several passages in the New Testament Gospels that need especially close examination. The first is John 6:40: "And this is the will of Him who sent me, that everyone who is beholding the Son, and is believing in him, may have life age-during, and I will raise him up in the last day" (Young's Literal Translation).

Alone among major translation versions (twenty-four available at biblehub.com), the two literals: Young's Literal (YLT) and the Berean Literal (BLB) have the correct present active participle for both: "[is] beholding" and "[is] believing." The first verb is "theoron," the Greek for "to see," not "looks on" or "looks to," as is in two of the most widely read translations: the NIV (New International Version) and the ESV (English Standard Version). This corruption of scripture implies that all that is required is to "relate to" or "rely on" the Son. No. The Master and the disciple must be living concurrently. The confirmation is four lines before, in John 6:36, where the Master says that these people *did* see and didn't believe, so he means to see *physically*, with eyes, not in their hearts or minds, or some other kind of "seeing." And the "seeing" is ongoing—'is beholding.' This is meditation—seeing the Master daily in his Radiant Form.

A similar statement of limitation is John 9:4–5: "We must work the works of him who sent me while it is day; night is coming, when no one can work. *As long as I am in the world,* I am the light of the world" (ESV). The Codex Sinaiticus, the earliest complete, or nearly complete, new Testament manuscript, has "sent us" for 9:4 (not "sent me"). Thus, Jesus is not exempting *himself* or the elect from "working while it is day [while he is alive]." He would not say "as long as I am in the world," even if the Comforter is to be sent, unless his ministry was time-dependent. It would only confuse those not yet born as to whether or not he was really their Master. A similar allied problem is not addressed in any meaningful way in the New Testament: What about those who were born and died *before* Jesus lived? Why were they born at all? They never knew about savior Jesus. They don't count?

Mark 10:45 is another misunderstood verse. "For even the Son of Man did not come to be served, but to serve, and to give His life a ransom for many" (ASV). The Greek word for life is "Psuchen" and means "soul," "breath,"or"self."Ithasn'tanythingtodowithdying. Thisverseisn'tabout death or dying. It is about giving life, while living. He says, "a ransom *for many.*" It wasn't a ransom *for all,* as a death ransom would have been— whether it be accepted or not. Others interpreted this as they wished, not as the Master who spoke it meant it to be understood. A translator's choice is whether to capitalize "His" in "His life." It is, technically, "His," as this is the Word, or Spirit form, of the Master—the Son, which is "His." The Spirit and Son are One. There is no Trinity. Son and Spirit are the same. Original Hebrew Matthew has no Trinity.

Many passages are simply misread within their context. "Rise, let us be going, my betrayer [Deliverer] is at hand" (Matt. 26:46, Mark 14:42) and "Rise, let us go hence" (John 14:31) are examples of mystic ascension that are misread. Whether it was done knowingly is unclear, but it seems possible. In the Synoptic tradition, Judas comes *immediately after* this declaration of the "Son of man delivered into the hands of sinners" [the disciples] by Jesus. That is because in the original quotation by a real Master, the statement is about rising within in spirit to meet the "Deliverer," who is now to be "Judas," the new Master, upon the transfer of spirit symbolized by the kiss in the original Gnostic tradition. So, it seems that this could well be a double meaning: the coming of the Holy Spirit to the disciples, and the coming of the new Master to them. They are to "seize" him spiritually, in the sense that "seize" is used in the Gnostic Apocalypses of James for the archons seizing James. The three denials—inverted—come next in the canon, from the context of the disciple Peter being "reproved" by Jesus for not working hard enough to concentrate in his meditation in the Apocalypse of Peter. Note that Jesus "comes" to the disciples *three* times in the context of prayer and "watching" (meditating) before the betrayal kiss in the canonical accounting, finding them "sleeping."

Mark 14:21, Matthew 26:24, and Luke 22:22 have variations of "For the Son of Man goes as it is written of him, but woe to that man by whom the Son of Man is betrayed! It would have been better for that man if he had not been born" (ESV). The "woe" is the "mourn deeply" or "grieve a great deal" (Meyer) of Gospel of Judas, 35:27. The initiate is going to leave himself *behind* and go forward in the spirit of the Master. The Greek word normally translated as "betrayed" is "paradidomi"— "to deliver." In many places, such as John 19:16, "Then he handed him over to be crucified" this is "hand over" or "deliver," which is the same word. This leaving oneself behind, the "woe to that man," is the equivalent of "Truly I say to you, this baptism which they received in my Name [...] will destroy the earthly man Adam. Tomorrow he who bears me will be tormented" (Gospel of Judas, 55:26–56:6). Letting go is not easily done – for anyone.

Mark 14:62 says, "And Jesus said, 'I am, and you will see the Son of Man seated at the right hand of Power, and coming with the clouds of heaven'" (ESV). This has been seen above as deriving directly from the Eusebius account of Hegesippus and James's saying, "Why ask ye me concerning Jesus the Son of man? He Himself sitteth in heaven, at the right hand of the Great Power, and shall come on the clouds of heaven."

There are two problematic prophecy passages in the betrayal: Matthew 26:31 (also related in Mark 14:26) and John 13:18. Both are mistranslations of the scriptural referent. "Then Jesus said to them, 'You will all fall away because of me this night. For it is written, "I will strike the shepherd, and the sheep of the flock will be scattered. This is simply a Christianized error. The LXX (Septuagint) was evidently completed by a later generation of Christian scribes, who made a mistake in translating this verse in the Tanakh. It is Zechariah 13:7. This is a completely misunderstood passage of deeply mystical meaning. Whatever the historical context, the literary and spiritual dynamic is very clear. There are bad shepherd-priests, and there is a good shepherd. The good shepherd leads the flock to union with the Lord. *He* is the one to do the "striking" in 13:7, refining the lucky third, the "little ones" in fire "as one refines silver." They will "call on my Name [the Apophasis Logos], and I will answer them. I will say, 'They are my people,' and they will say, 'The Lord is my God.'" This is the ending of the good shepherd-bad shepherds pericope that begins with the bad shepherds at Zechariah 10:2: "Therefore the people wander like sheep; they are afflicted for want of a shepherd."

The opening of the poetic segment of the pericope is 11:1–3 (RSV):

> Open your doors, O, Lebanon, that the fire may devour your cedars!
> Wail, O cypress, for the cedar has fallen, for the glorious trees are ruined!
> Hark, the wail of the shepherds, for their glory is despoiled!
> Hark, the roar of the lions, for the jungle of the Jordan is laid waste!

It doesn't take much of a sleuth to see that shortly thereafter, at 13:7–9, the form is repeated:

> "Awake, O sword of my shepherd, against the man who stands next to me," says the Lord of hosts.

> Strike the shepherd [O, shepherd] that the sheep may be

scattered. I will turn my hand against the little ones.

In the whole land, says the Lord, two thirds shall be cut off and perish, and one third shall be left alive.

And I will put this third into the fire, and refine them as one refines silver, and test them as gold is tested.

They will call on my name, and I will answer them. I will say, "They are my people"; and they will say, "The Lord is my God."

There is so much to be said about this "flock doomed to slaughter." Firstly, their "slaughter" is *a good thing.* Their "refining as in fire" is a *good* thing. "Devouring the flesh of the fat ones, tearing off even their hooves" (11:16) is a *good* thing. This is the *good* shepherd at work, the little ones "sacrificing the man that bears them" as they cooperate. A clue to this is 13:6: "And if one asks him, 'What are these wounds on your back?' he will say, 'The wounds I received in the house of my friend.'" This is not correct. The Hebrew is "yad," or "yadecha," and "bayin," or "bayn," for "hands" and "between," respectively—translated in the RSV as "back" and "on." "Friend," or "lover," is "aheb." The wounds that the "tiller of the soil" prophet received at the house of his beloved are *"between the hands,"* not "on your back," "on your chest," "on the arms," or any of the other poor translations. The "wounds" are *"between the hands."* This, let it be recalled, is the "hands raised" in meditation (Apocalypse of Peter), placed on the head so as to see within and hear the sound within. The "wounds" are the "striking" of the Master at the "single eye" or "mind's eye" of Matthew 6:22, "between" the hands placed beside the head and across the forehead in meditation position. Refer to Hosea 6:1-2: "In their affliction they will rise early to me: Come, and let us return to the Lord: For he hath taken us, and he will heal us: *he will strike,* and he will cure us" (DRB).

This is mysticism at its deepest. There is no doubt about it. The

Hebrew demands it, and Zechariah demands it. The Master is the good shepherd, coming to "refine the flock" by "striking the sheep" with the "sword of his mouth" (Rev.1:16,19:15): "Awake, O sword of my shepherd, within the man who is my companion," says the Lord of hosts. "Strike, O shepherd, that the sheep may be shattered, and I will replace my hand upon the little ones."

This one case of mistranslation corrected is, by itself, a major contribution to the understanding of not just the New Testament but the mystic understanding of all scripture. As far as this author is aware, there is no other commentator who has offered this correction. The proof is 13:6. The Hebrew "yad bayin," or "yadecha bayn," is quite obviously misconstrued in all extant versions. So is "strike *the* shepherd." The poetic structure of "O this" and "O that" in evidence at 11:1–2 is undeniable. It occurs elsewhere in the Old Testament (Tanakh): Numbers 24:5 and Isaiah1:2. It recurs at Zechariah 13:7. Poetic repetition is a common form in this literature. The symmetry of the good-bad shepherds pericope demands it, if not the mystic correctness of the reading. This author's first book contains a thorough examination of this verse. The "mark of the accusative," Hebrew "et," is allowed for cases like this of "introduction of a new subject."[44] The Hebrew "utepusena" from the root "puwts" (Strong's # 6327) is literally "shattered" in pieces, which fits this verse better than the normal "scattered." Hence, another mistranslation of this verse. Zechariah 13:7 is not support for Matthew 26:31/Mark 14:26. It does not support a Christian martyred savior figure. It describes the spiritual salvation of the disciples of *a living Master.*

An equally important mistaken translation is John 13:18's quotation of Psalm 41:9. For months this author pondered how this verse could be correctly used in John 13:18. It comes as an apparent negative in the middle of another wise entirely positive passage on succession in John13: "I know whom *I have chosen*" (13:18a) and "he who receives *the one* whom I send receives me" (13:20a, ESV).

---

44   Francis Brown, *Brown-Driver-Briggs Hebrew and English Lexicon,* (Hendrickson Publishers, Peabody, Mass., 2012), 85.

"I am not speaking of all of you; I know whom I have chosen. But the Scripture will be fulfilled, 'He who ate my bread has lifted his heel against me'" (13:18, ESV). This is a wrong use of Psalm 41:9. Incorrectly, it is the literal translation of a Hebrew idiomatic saying: "For even the man of peace, in whom I trusted, who ate my bread, hath greatly supplanted me" (DRB). The Catholic version, curiously, is *the only one* to get this translation correctly. Even though the sense of the passage is still somewhat negative, in that "supplant" has the connotation of force, the replacement dynamic is what is important here. In the story of Isaac's inheritance co- opted, Jacob and Esau contest for succession (not the standard assumption here of Ahithophel and David, and a case of betrayal). Jacob grasps Esau "by the heel," Hebrew "aqeb" (Strong's #6119). "Aqeb" has the root letters for "Ya'aqov," Hebrew for the Greek "Jacob" and the English "James." Here we have a replacement of the Master speaking in John 13 about succession with someone named "James." More coverage of this verse can be found in the author's first book. It is apparent that the author of John knew the real meaning of the Hebrew and was making clever use of the confusion in his diversionary portrayal of Judas as the betrayer. The English Standard Version translation of "ho" (Strong's # 3588), meaning "the one" sent, is important, as it shows the way word choices like "whomsoever I send" (KJV) and "anyone I send" (NIV) can corrupt the passage. This 'one' is extremely important, as Jesus sent just *one* successor—"ho" (Greek for "*the* one"). Only "Judas," the "chosen" one, received the bread (John 13:27)— James—in Gospel of the Hebrews, as we shall soon see.

John 13 as Mysticism

The following John 13 passage is taken from the English Standard Version:

> [1]Now before the Feast of the Passover, when Jesus knew that his hour had come to depart out of this world to the Father, having loved his own who were in the world, he loved them to the end.

The beloved, John says, "his own *who were in the world,"* were categorically not those *yet to be born or those who had already died.* John 17:11 is the same, in Jesus's own words.

> [2]During supper, when the devil had already put it into the heart of Judas Iscariot, Simon's son, to betray him, [3]Jesus, knowing that the Father had given all things into his hands, and that he had come from God and was going back to God, [4]rose from supper. He laid aside his outer garments, and taking a towel, tied it around his waist.[5] Then he poured water into a basin and began to wash the disciples' feet and to wipe them with the towel that was wrapped around him. [6]He came to Simon Peter, who said to him, "Lord, do you wash my feet?" [7]Jesus answered him, "What I am doing you do not understand now, but afterward you will understand."

> [8]Peter said to him, "You shall never wash my feet." Jesus answered him, "If I do not wash you, you have no share with me."

Maharaj Charan Singh writes, "This has a beautiful mystic meaning. Unless the Master washes away our sins, we cannot merge in him and cannot go back to the Father. But when we do the spiritual practice according to his instructions, we clear our karmas, we get rid of all our sins. The more sins we have, the longer it takes, but ultimately we become pure and merge in the Shabd, which is the real form of the Master. Then we are part of him who has merged in the Father."[45]

> [9]Simon Peter said to him, "Lord, not my feet only but also my hands and my head!"

> [10]Jesus said to him, "The one who has bathed does not need to wash, except for his feet, but is completely clean. And you are clean, but not every one of you."

---

[45] Singh, Charan, *Light on St. John* (Radha Soami Satsang beas, 1967), 190.

Interpreted by a Master: "The Master himself is 'clean every whit' because he has no karmas or sins of his own 'save to wash his feet,' which means all the karmas that he has taken on himself for the benefit of his disciples and which he can easily wash off when he sees fit to do so. 'And ye [my disciples] are clean', says Christ, 'but not all.' Since you are attached to the Word, you are in the process of being cleansed. In other words, you have been cleansed to a certain extent by coming on the path, but you have yet to make a lot of spiritual progress before you can become absolutely pure to merge in the Word, the Holy Ghost, the real form of the Master within you."[46]

> [11]For he knew who was to betray him; that was why he said, "Not all of you are clean."
>
> [12]When he had washed their feet and put on his outer garments and resumed his place, he said to them, "Do you understand what I have done to you?
>
> [13]"You call me Teacher and Lord, and you are right, for so I am."

"He says: No doubt you address me as 'Master,' no doubt you address me as 'Lord,' and there is nothing wrong with it, because I am the Master, I am the Lord; but you have not washed yourself yet. You do not have as much faith in me as you should have."[47]

> [14]If I then, your Lord and Teacher, have washed your feet, you also ought to wash one another's feet. [15]For I have given you an example, that you also should do just as I have done to you. [16]Truly, truly, I say to you, a servant is not greater than his master, nor is a messenger greater than the one who sent him. [17]If you know these things, blessed are you

---

[46]

[47]   Singh, Light on St. John, 191.

if you do them.[18] I am not speaking of all of you; I know
whom I have chosen. But the Scripture will be fulfilled,
"He who ate my bread has lifted his heel against me."

"Christ says: I am appointing only one of you to succeed me as Master.
It is mentioned in all the scriptures that a living Master is necessary to
put those in touch with the Word who are ready and marked by the
Father. Since I shall soon be leaving you, I am appointing a successor
to look after those whom I have initiated and will also initiate the souls
allotted to him by the Lord: so again there will be one shepherd and
one fold, as ordained by the Father."[48]

[19]I am telling you this now, before it takes place, that when
it does take place you may believe that I am he.[20] Truly, truly,
I say to you, whoever receives the one I send receives me,
and whoever receives me receives the one who sent me.

Finally, from Master Charan Singh: "Again Christ is speaking to
them about his successor. He says: Now while I am in the flesh I am
trying to guide you and to tell you that soon I shall be leaving you. I
also want you to know that I am appointing a successor and that there
is no difference between him and me. For you, I am in my successor
and my successor is in me. And for those whom he initiates, he is in
the Father and the Father is in him. It all amounts to the same thing,
for we are all one. All realized souls are one in the Father and the Father
is in them.

"Whomever recognizes as my successor that person whom I shall
appoint to carry on the teachings, will actually be showing love and
faith in me, because it is my wish that you look upon me as your Master
while I am in the flesh [italics original]. Since I and my Father are one,
you will also be honoring the Father by loving and respecting the one
whom I shall select to guide you.[49]

---

[48]   Singh, *Light on St. John*, 192.
[49]

> [21]After saying these things, Jesus was troubled in his spirit, and testified, "Truly, truly, I say to you, one of you will betray me."

"Paradidomi" is Greek for "to deliver," not "to be tray." The context is what Jesus is saying, *not* what John is writing.

> [22]The disciples looked at one another, uncertain of whom he spoke. [23]One of his disciples, whom Jesus loved, was reclining at table at Jesus' side,[24]so Simon Peter motioned to him to ask Jesus of whom he was speaking. [25]So that disciple, leaning back against Jesus, said to him, "Lord, who is it?"

John 13:24 is an extremely important verse for understanding the entire "betrayal." The verb "pythesthai" (Strong's #4441) is translated as either "tell" or "ask," depending on the version. It makes a *big* difference. It can be either a command or a request: "So Simon Peter beckoned to him and said, 'Tell us who it is of whom he speaks.'" That's the RSV. The King James Version has "Simon Peter therefore beckoned to him that he should ask who it should be of whom he spake." Those are two very different sentences. Why would Peter be asking *Judas* to ask Jesus who is the betrayer of Christ? One has Peter asking Judas *to tell them* who is traitor (or successor), and the other has Peter asking Judas *to ask Jesus* who it is. One wouldn't expect a traitor to reveal himself, and the scribes knew it. They changed the verb form in the less accurate manuscript source for the King James Version. This telltale change to "pythesthai" is also one way to see that the beloved disciple was James, not John. The beloved disciple had a higher status than Peter. Peter motioning to the beloved disciple was a sign of deference. Peter asked James who the successor was because he figured it was to be James! He deferred—as he should—to the favored disciple to answer it. "Judas," not yet the Master, asked Jesus who it was. Peter asking Judas to ask Jesus who the betrayer was is an orthodox corruption of the tradition. Peter *commanded him* to tell who it was! This is an example of why the RSV translators relied, and rightly so, on the more reliable Nestle-Aland (Novum Testamentum Graece) manuscript and not the KJV Latin Vulgate.

> [26]Jesus answered, "It is he to whom I will give this morsel of bread when I have dipped it." So when he had dipped the morsel, he gave it to Judas, the son of Simon Iscariot. [27]Then after he had taken the morsel, Satan entered into him. Jesus said to him, "What you are going to do, do quickly." [28]Now no one at the table knew why he said this to him. [29]Some thought that, because Judas had the money bag, Jesus was telling him, "Buy what we need for the feast," or that he should give something to the poor. [30]So, after receiving the morsel of bread, he immediately went out. And it was night. [31]When he had gone out, Jesus said, "Now is the Son of Man glorified, and God is glorified in him. [32]If God is glorified in him, God will also glorify him in himself, and glorify him at once. [33]Little children, yet a little while I am with you. You will seek me, and just as I said to the Jews, so now I also say to you, 'Where I am going you cannot come.'"

The Gospel of John 13:31 (Gospel of Judas 56:22-58:6) says, *"Now is the Son of Man glorified."* When 'he [Judas] had gone out,' Judas [*James*] was "now" the new Master, and "God is glorified *in him.*" The Son of Man is James—not Jesus (nor Judas)! Jesus immediately says that he is "yet a little while" with them. Jesus, therefore, cannot be the subject of glorification here, as he was supposedly to be glorified by *dying*. God is "glorified in him," *James*—the one who has "gone out." God is not "glorified in him," *Jesus*—a good long while from "now."

> [34]"A new commandment I give to you, that you love one another: just as I have loved you, you also are to love one

74

another. ³⁵By this all people will know that you are my
disciples, if you have love for one another."

³⁶Simon Peter said to him, "Lord, where are you going?"
Jesus answered him, "Where I am going you cannot follow
me now, but you will follow afterward." ³⁷Peter said to him,
"Lord, why can I not follow you now? I will lay down my
life for you." ³⁸Jesus answered, "Will you lay down your
life for me? Truly, truly, I say to you, the rooster will not
crow till you have denied me three times.

Peter is then denied ("reproved") by Jesus *three times* in the original
gnostic version, and also *"in this night,"* (Apocalypse of Peter 72:2–3).
Being the successor to James, Peter is also subject to the ridicule of the
proto-orthodoxy.

One other note about chapter 13: "Now before the feast of the
Passover, when Jesus knew that his hour had come to depart out of this
world to the Father, *having loved his own who were in the world,* he loved
them to the end" (13:1). If Jesus were really the savior for all people of
all times, would John ever say such a thing? Or consider John 17:11:
"And now I am no more in the world, *but they are in the world,* and I am
coming to thee." Would Jesus really say something like this about his
"chosen" in the world if "they" were not *all* of them? "*As long as I am in
the world,* I am the Light of the world" (John 9:5). He limits himself
and his power to his own time. "We must do the works of Him who
sent us while it is day; night comes, when *no one* can work" (John 9:4,
Codex Sinaiticus original wording "sent us").

John 14:22 says, "Judas (not Iscariot⁵⁰) said to him, 'Lord, how is
it that you will manifest yourself to us, and not to the world?' Jesus
answered him, 'If a man loves me, he will keep my Word, and my Father
will love him, and we will come to him, and make our home with him.
He who does not love me does not keep my *words*; and *the Word which
you hear* is not mine but the Father's who sent me." The Greek for both

---

⁵⁰   Note that this is Judas "not Iscariot"—yet another cover character for James.

instances of "word" here is "logos," singular in the final telling usage. This is the Divine Word they are hearing, not the "rhema," or spoken word. Curiously, Jesus says "we will come." That's the Word and the Master "coming." This passage is not in the betrayal narrative section, but since John says it is "Judas" (but maybe "not Iscariot"!), it should be seen as related. It is part of the "I am" dynamic in John and came from the Gnostic concept of the indwelling Logos. James is now the Master, the pillar upon which the world balances or, as the Gospel of Thomas puts it, the one "for whom heaven and earth were created."

Both of these key verses above, Matthew 26:41 and John 13:18, once translated correctly, completely torpedo any idea of a real betrayal. If the authors must go to such lengths to get material, it means there must be something wrong with the story. But there is more. Even the grammar is wrong in some cases. Besides the continuous present tense in the Greek for all of John's salvation verses, such as 6:40 and 12:44, routinely mistranslated in all but the Young's Literal Translation, there are wholesale grammatical errors in such verses as John 18:9–10. If one simply goes to biblehub.com, one will see that the Greek words "hina" and "oun" are the conjunctions that lead off these two verses. The first, "hina," is the subordinate conjunction, translated "that," as in biblehub.com Greek text analysis:

STRONGS NT 2443: "hina"

Strong's Concordance
hina: in order that, that, so that
Part of Speech: Conjunction
Transliteration: hina
Short Definition: in order that, so that

Definition: in order that, so that (a subordinating conjunction)–for the purpose that (in order that), looking to the aim (intended result) of the verbal idea.
Word Origin: a prim. conjunction denoting purpose, definition or result.

And the second, "oun," is the adverbial conjunction "therefore," as in:
STRONGS NT 3767: "oun"

Strong's Concordance
oun: therefore, then, (and) so
Part of Speech: Conjunction
Transliteration: oun
Short Definition: therefore, then
Definition: therefore, then.

Thayer's Greek Lexicon

3767 oun—a conjunction indicating that something follows from another necessarily. Hence, it is used in drawing a conclusion and in connecting sentences together logically, then, therefore, accordingly, consequently, these things being so.

What this all means is that John 18:9 is dependent on 18:10. They are *connected* linguistically and, in fact, are properly one sentence: "That the word of the Lord be fulfilled, 'Of those whom thou gavest me I lost not one;' therefore, Peter, having a sword, drew it and struck the high priest's slave and cut off his right ear. The slave's name was Malchus." The adverb "oun" leading off 18:10 is a conjunctive adverb, and it is correctly "therefore," not "then," following, as it does, the subordinate, "that" of 18:9. The translator's improper choice of the usual rendering, "then," was made in an obviously orthodox corruption of scripture. One can even see the continuing corruptive tendencies in Christendom in the recent translation versions, such as the NIV: "This happened so that…,"a blatant attempt to force the subordinate clause to refer to the arrest. At least the early versions leave it uncommitted with simply, "that"—and a sentence without a proper verb, as the KJV does. One can see right away that the Greek has nothing to do with the previous action, which is the prophesied arrest of Jesus, but is in fact a foretelling of the cutting of the right ear of Malchus, the high priest's slave. But why would the prophesy of John 17:12, "that none should be lost," be about Malchus? Because this is a symbolic initiation. The sword of Peter is symbolic of the initiating power of Peter (probably James, however, since he is the successor. Unnamed in Matthew, John is the only Gospel to name this "one of those who were with Jesus" wielding a sword, whose obfuscation is a good indication that it was really James.)

The fact that it is the *right ear* is enormously significant. It isn't just "cut off his ear" but "cut off *his right ear.*" In modern mystic teaching, students are taught that there are two spiraling spiritual currents within the body (please refer to the Staff of Caduceus), one ascending and one descending (John 1:51, with "Son of man" as the Spirit, and also in the "loaves and fishes" feeding-of-the-multitude story, where the fishes are symbolic of these energy currents).[51] It is the right side with which one "hears" the ascending Shabd, Logos, or Word, the "Name of the Lord." Jesus "touches" the ear, but heals "*him*" (Luke22:51), not the ear! He heals Malchus spiritually, not physically. Malchus was the final initiate of Jesus, not the first initiate of "Peter." It says in John 18:11, "Jesus said to Peter, 'Peter, put your sword into its sheath; shall I not drink the cup which the Father has given me?'" This "cup" is trouble. It is the cup of sins, or karmas, that Malchus brings to the Master. Jesus is asking Peter why he should not assume the sins of his initiate, Malchus, and save his soul. After all, would Jesus really think that one of "his" should be "lost" *if arrested?* No. He was concerned about his disciples' *spiritual* well-being, not merely their worldly freedom, and certainly not his own—which is the real reason why he allowed himself to be "arrested" or "seized" *spiritually (by his disciples).* This is the story of *their* deliverance.

There is still more of interest in John 18. In John 18:6, the arresting party comes to Jesus and asks for him: "When therefore he said to them, 'I am he', *they drew back* and fell to the ground." After

---

51   Stone, *Mystic Bible*, 187.

he answers them, there is the phrase, in Greek, "apelthon eis ta opiso." This is grammatically most properly a case of them withdrawing inside, spiritually: "they withdrew back in." As strange as this may sound, it is perfectly in keeping with "of those whom thou gavest me, I lost not one" and "should I not drink the cup which the Father has given me?" 'James (as Judas) was bringing Malchus to Jesus for initiation (and some others, evidently, as it is plural: "they" withdrew). Having "withdrawn inside" or withdrawn their consciousness, "they fell to the ground"—as would be expected of one having a profound realization upon seeing the Master within. From the start, this "seizing the Master" is about initiation. John cleverly used the occasion of the betrayal to overwrite the initiation of Malchus, his final disciple. (The thief on the cross saved is purely fictional.) As noted earlier, a passage of this withdrawal of consciousness is seen in the Gnostic book, *Thomas the Contender*, from the Nag Hammadi collection: "They will withdraw from their limbs not patiently [through meditation], but with despair [upon dying]" (141:37–8). The guards "trembling" and "becoming like dead men" in Matthew 28:4 is this same process of withdrawal of consciousness, overwritten by the empty-tomb fiction. (A probable source is "Bring me from a tomb alive"— Second Apocalypse of James 63:5.)

The Synoptics even confirm that the "sword" in John 18 is a sword of spiritual power. Both Mark and Matthew have the arresting party "laying on hands and seizing him" after the kiss but before the sword strikes Malchus. Luke 22:49, however, has the disciples asking, "Lord, shall we strike with the sword?" coming after the phrase, "And when those who were about him saw what would follow…" Is this James "following" Jesus as Master? The sword "striking" query is in the same relative position as "they laid hands on him and seized him," which sounds curiously like a spiritual apprehending of the new Master, preceded as it is with the kiss of Jesus by "Judas" (James). This would be the disciples asking Jesus if the new Master is to begin initiations. The cutting of Malchus' right ear follows. We know that that is initiation. It would not be possible to see these connections were it not for the Nag Hammadi discovery. Taken altogether, the many parallels of the canon to the Nag Hammadi Apocalypses simply cannot be coincidence, and they must be original to the Gnostics who wrote them. What sense does the betrayal story make? It has been a problem for apologists since the beginning. And the scholars' backward thinking on what the Gospel of Judas means is even more pathetic. Nag Hammadi should be regarded as the new information that it is, shedding light on a very old story.

Also, in John 18:14, Jesus, Lazarus, and Judas can be seen as covers for James in, "Caiaphas had given counsel to the Jews that it was expedient that one man ['Jesus'] should die for the people," John 12:10–11 says, "So the chief priests planned to put Lazarus also to death, because on account of him many of the Jews were going away and believing on Jesus." This informs Luke 16 by way of the parable of Lazarus and the rich man, where the rich man, "Caiaphas," upon dying, sees Abraham and asks him to send Lazarus to his five brothers to save them from hell. The "five brothers" are the sons-in-law of "Caiaphas" (all high priests coming one after the other, culminating in Ananus ben Ananus, the high priest who condemned James). Lazarus, targeted by the high priests in John for elimination "because on account of him many of the Jews were going away and believing on Jesus" is connected to James through Hegesippus (via Eusebius). The high priests demanded that James repudiate faith in Jesus because "those who did come to believe did so because of James."

"Lazarus" is, therefore, James. James refused to repudiate Jesus and was attacked by the Scribes and Pharisees (Hegesippus). The trial and death of Jesus for blasphemy then parallels the trial and death of James (Caiaphas and Ananas ben Ananus each conducting illegal trials, and a mob of Jews calling for the death of each). James ("Lazarus") is "the beloved disciple" from John 11:35–36, the one on Jesus's breast (and for whom Jesus "wept" upon hearing of his death in John 11:35), the one asked by Peter to ask Jesus who will deliver Jesus. The beloved disciple is James because it is James who "delivers" Jesus (they "believed on Jesus because of him") in Hegesippus. James is also the beloved disciple in John from information in the Gnostic texts because he is the successor, and "Judas" is James, who receives the bread. The beloved disciple/ Lazarus/Judas/James receives the bread at the Last Supper according to the now-lost Gospel of the Hebrews (this by way of church fathers Papias, Jerome, and Eusebius).[52]

One further cover-up by the church is the assertion that the Prologue of John ,John1:1–18, is all about Jesus. It is not. John 1:6–13 is about the Master John the Baptist, giving "power to become children of God."[53] Jesus is not mentioned until 1:14 by way of 1:15. A "Baptist" is one who baptizes, and John was a baptizing Master, every bit the equal to Jesus Christ, whomever he might have been. In so many ways is John the Baptist minimized that another book (the author's first book) was necessary to handle them all. Suffice it to say that Jesus himself calls John the "greatest born of woman" (Matt.11:11). The "he that is least" addition is yet another orthodox corruption. Jesus is also quoted as saying, "You were willing to rejoice for a season in his light" (John 5:35). Who "rejoices" for a herald, less than a savior, and who has "light" but a Master?

Acts

Luke's Acts is a fitting place to close our canonical investigation of Judas. Here you have the genesis of it, with Dr. Robert Eisenman's provocative assertion of Judas as a cover for James in Acts 1 and Stephen as a cover for James in Acts 7:37 (*James the Brother of Jesus*). From these two stunning bits of Eisenman genius, this present author simply moved over to the Gospels to see what might be hidden there. This short, but hopefully game-changing, book is the result.

Judas dies in two ways in the New Testament, depending on which author you read. Read from Matthew, and he hangs himself (27:5). Read from Luke and he falls to a gory death in a field (Acts 1:18). He can't die both ways, and the other Gospel authors don't help much. They skip the whole scene. There are even attempts to harmonize

---

52   Throckmorton and Barnstone, "Early Christian Writings: Gospel of the Hebrews," accessed August 19, 2016, http://www.earlychristianwritings.com/text/ gospelhebrews-throck.html.

53   Singh, Light on St. John, 19.

these two disparate accounts, and at least one is online, by a Ph.D. apologist at "Answers in Genesis." Judas is said by Luke to have fallen "headlong" (Acts 1:18, and similarly in Clement's Recognitions 1:70), so if he hanged himself as well, it must have been *by his feet.* Do you really believe this, Dr. Georgia Purdom? All one can say is we hope this book finds you soon.

Dr. Eisenman mentions that Acts 1:21 does not fit Judas but does fit James. There is no "office" of apostle, but there is an office (RSV) of the Bishoprick (KJV). James was the first "bishop" of the Jerusalem Assembly. And Joseph Barsabbas *Justus,* a peculiar name for the defeated candidate to replace Judas in the drawing of straws (another fabrication from a prior script), just happens to be the Latin equivalent of James *the Just.* Matthias, the one to replace Judas, is someone never heard from before and thus not likely to have "been with them since the beginning" (Acts 1:22). He is also never heard from again in Acts or in the Gospel of Judas, surprisingly enough! Paul has Jesus risen appearing—to the "twelve" (1Cor.15:5), not eleven, so Judas is not missing for Paul—as if he ever heard of him anyway. This is all as phony as a three-dollar bill.

In Acts 7, the details of the stoning of the archetypal Gentile Christian, "Stephen," are all significant for James. He is said to have been "cast out" by his accusers (1), "praying," "kneeling down," and "crying out" (2,3,4) with "garments at the feet of Saul" (Paul) in a sign of his involvement (5), stoned for blasphemy (6), while saying, "Lord, do not hold this sin against them," which is what Hegesippus says James said (7) (Acts 7:54–60). All these details are associated with the life and death of James the Just in historical sources. The final line, Acts 8:1, even admits, "And Saul was consenting to his death" as in Pseudoclementine Recognitions 1:70. Why was Luke hiding James (again, as in Acts 1 and in Luke)?

Richard Pervo does a magnificent job of showing the fabrication of stories in Acts, as does Dr. Eisenman, in his book *The Mystery of Acts.*[54] *Gospel Fictions* by Randel Helms does the same for the four Gospels.[55]

---

[54]   Richard Pervo, The Mystery of Acts (Polebridge Press, Santa Rosa, 2008).

[55]   Randel Helms, Gospel Fictions (Prometheus Books, Amherst, NY, 1988).

William Klassenon Judas and Mark 14:21, "Woe to that man"

Within the biblical scholarly community we find the distinguished research professor William Klassen, Canadian professor of early Christian literature at Toronto University, University of Waterloo, and the Ecole Biblique at Jerusalem. In *Judas, Betrayer or Friend of Jesus?*, Klassen— noting that all lists of the disciples include Judas, a mark of importance "according to Jewish custom"—writes, "It cannot be ruled out, however, that he [Judas] understood better than any other disciple the need for Jesus to be 'handed over' and was prepared to follow the directions of Jesus in this act as well. In any case, 'a man whom the redeemer has thus distinguished merits the best interpretation we can give of his acts.'"[56]

"To Mark and his community, Judas is of little direct interest: he is simply the one who 'handed over' (Mark 3:19, 14:10, 43). By name he appears only three times."[57] Well, we now know why: James needed to be hidden. It wasn't a case of "the criterion of embarrassment" barring an invented Judas. He was necessary to hide the real Master, James, so the nascent church could grow without interference.

Regarding the "woe to that man" of Mark 14:21: "We must guard against any equation of the woe with a curse. A woe in ancient Judaism was an expression of love. Just as the prophets spoke their woes to the people of Israel in ancient days, so Jesus spoke his woes to those who would live with the reversals the kingdom brings. He had a special concern for the informer, without whom apparently he could not carry out his mission, but whose participation most certainly would lead to woes. Any reading of this saying other than a cry of compassion from the Master on behalf of one of his disciples is a serious misreading of the text [Mark 14:21]. . . . *Woe cries are evident among the traditions of the just man* [italics added]. . . . The woe is meant to bring someone to repentance. It's very passionate cry is meant to awaken people to the reality of their condition."[57] That is some amazing insight from an

---

56   William Klassen, Judas, Betrayer or Friend of Jesus? (Fortress Press, Minneapolis, 1996), 38.

57   Ibid., 79.

orthodox investigator. Luke, in contrast to Matthew and Mark, omits "better for that man if he had not been born" in an admission that this is not a condemnation of Judas. Note that this woe in the Synoptics' "handing over" is equivalent to "you will *exceed them all*, for you will sacrifice the man who bears me." The "condition" in question, Dr. Klassen, is that of a disciple's deep devotion, to the point of total self-sacrifice! The Jesus 'prophecy' of Mark 9:31 that he would be handed over, was "to men"—not "to sinners" as in Mark 14. Thus, the sinful disciples (i.e., Judas) is a later tradition, the original being more in line with the gnostic "handing over" to devoted disciples.

"To assume that Jesus curses Judas confuses the very clear words employed by the New Testament to describe curses. Jesus instructed his disciples to 'bless those who curse you' (Luke 6:28); it would hardly be the case that he would curse one of his own disciples. He no more curses 'the deliverer' here than he does the women who are expectant with child or suckling during the hard times, connected with the abomination of desolation (Mark 13:17)."[58] "Matthew's preference for direct discourse signifies something about his style, but it is also a mark of early Christian literature, *especially Gospels* [italics added]."[59] The Gospel of Judas is a direct discourse gospel.

"It would have violated a fundamental rule of Judaism if Jesus had told Judas to commit a sin [on passages such as John 13:27]. Can we really say that Jesus allowed his fellow Jew to write a passage ticket to hell?"[60]

"The kiss is an affirmation of covenant faithfulness."[61]

And as for Judas being possessed by a "demon," Dr. DeConick, Klassen has this to say: "Mark makes no connection between Judas's act and the demonic."[62] "Was Judas not to be saved from Satan as others were?"[63] Whatever happened to "casting out" of "demons"?

---

58   Ibid., 83–84.

59   Ibid., 83.

60   Ibid., 111.

61   Ibid., 111.

62   Ibid., 90.

63   Ibid., 143.

William Klassen clearly is not one to be found in the "traitor Judas" camp. His Judas is a disciple merely trying to do the will of his Master.

John Kloppenborg on Q and Early Salvation Theology

John Kloppenborg is another University of Toronto biblical scholar who has helpful insight into early Gnostic salvation theology. Kloppenborg's short but fascinating look at *Quelle* ('Source'), in *Q, the Earliest Gospel*, is further support for an early tradition of a Gnostic salvation, not a martyred Jesus salvation:

"If it is correct that Q 13:35 (Q mostly tracks Luke: "You will not see me until you say 'Blessed is the one who comes in the name of the Lord'") invokes the concept of assumption rather than resurrection, we can suggest that the Q people regarded Jesus' death as the death of a just man or a prophet whom God had 'taken up,' pending some future eschatological function. This accounts for the fact *that Q accords Jesus' death no special significance*, but jumps immediately to Jesus' return as the one who is to come (11:49, 13:34–35). In the parallel texts from Second Temple Judaism, it was not the death of the sage that was salvific, but rather the figure's expected eschatological role that was important [italics added]."[64] "[With the discovery of *The Gospel of Thomas*,] no longer was is it necessary to imagine that Q was a supplement of the passion kerygma [theme]. Q could well represent *a discrete and autonomous type of early Christian theologizing*, and ultimately be a gospel in its own right [italics added]."[65] This "theologizing" source for the canon—Q—like *Thomas* and its wisdom sayings, was Gnostic theology of wisdom salvation, not martyrdom salvation. What John Kloppenborg sees in Q is a clear case of an early gnosticizing influence on the canonical Gospels. The passion fiction with a salvific death on the cross came later.

G. A. Wells on "betrayal"

---

[64]   John Kloppenborg, *Q, the Earliest Gospel* (Westminster John Knox Press, Louisville, 2008), 84.

[65]   Ibid, 107.

G.A. Wells invites alternative solutions to the problem of 'the Betrayal': "For the earliest Christians, Jesus was 'delivered up' because this was part of God's plan to save mankind. Not until the Gospels is the 'delivering' given a historical context. Judas is said to 'deliver' him to the chief priests; the latter 'delivered' him to Pilate, who in turn 'delivered' him to soldiers for execution. The gospels have made the 'delivering up' into a series of precisely specified historical situations; and the RSV has allowed what the gospels say about Judas' betrayal to influence its rendering of Paul's statement [1 Cor. 11:23].

"The gospel story of Judas' betrayal is certainly fiction. Standard Christian works of reference admit that what he betrayed and why he betrayed are insoluble problems. Far from being too unedifying to be a Christian invention, the incident is typical of fiction where a superlatively great hero is betrayed by a false friend, as with King Arthur, Roland, Siegfried, and many others."[66]
Hyam Maccoby on Judas

The king of writers about the mythical Judas has to be Hyam Maccoby (1924-2004). His book, *Judas Iscariot and the Myth of Jewish Evil* (Free Press, New York, NY, 1992) is too good to be merely quoted. It is, rather, recommended to be read in its entirety for a genuinely Jewish viewpoint on the impossibility of a 'traitor' Judas Iscariot.

---

[66]   G. A Wells, *The Historical Evidence for Jesus* (Prometheus, Amherst, NY,1988), 26.

IV

Other Sources of Support for Mystic Readings of Scripture

Apocryphal support for the mystic reading of the canon is widespread. What follows is just a small sampling. The key to recognizing a mystic original tradition in whatever source is to compare ancient sources to recent works of mysticism. As we saw with "woe to that man," the true mystic interpretation is often not the superficial one.

Gospel of the Hebrews, Gospel According to Hebrew Matthew, Gospel of the Nazaraeans

The "bread" (as given to Judas, John 13:26, before the ascension, and mentioned above) *goes to James* in the Gospel of the Hebrews, according to Jerome (among others):

> The Gospel of the Nazaraeans ("observers") in Hebrew is believed to have been the Hebrew Gospel of Matthew and the source for the present gospel (which was composed in Greek). There are reliable witnesses that this gospel was both used and circulated among the earliest followers of Yahshua in the diaspora. Some believe it originated in Egypt and that the latest possible date it was written was during the first half of the second century; however, others believe that it was composed in the middle of the first century, when "Jesus" traditions were first being produced and collected. An earlier date is more likely than a later

one. Jerome, Eusebius, and Hegesippus (the latter two not quoting it) make mention of it, as do Origen and Clement (both Alexandrians). It is believed that Papias, who died about 130 C.E., knew of it and may have quoted it in his lost "Exegesis of the Sayings of the Lord." It is significant to note that Nicephorus, when drawing up his list of canonical and apocryphal books, stated that the Gospel of the Hebrews contained only 2200 lines, 300 fewer than Matthew. It has been suggested that these three hundred lines are the birth narratives of the first and second chapters of our canonical Matthew.

Jerome, On Illustrious Men, 2; (De viris in lustribus 2): Also the Gospel according to the Hebrews, which Origen often uses—recently translated by me into Greek and Latin—says, after the resurrection of the Savior, "Now the Lord, when he had given the linen cloth to the servant of the priest, went to James and appeared to him (for James had sworn that he would not eat bread from that hour in which he had drunk the Lord's cup until he should see him risen from among them that sleep)." And a little further on the Lord says, "Bring a table and bread." And immediately it is added, "He took bread and blessed and broke and gave it to James the Just and said to him, 'My brother, eat your bread, for the Son of man is risen from among them that sleep.'[67]

Compare Mark 14:25 (or Matthew 26:29) and note that the eating of bread is for James here—and not until his "Lord" has "risen from among them that sleep" rather than at the 'Last Supper.'

Equally important is the "linen cloth" removed here. This corresponds to Mark 14:51–52 and the "naked young man" who "flees" (rises) after shedding his garment, seen as well in the Second Apocalypse of James.

---

[67]   Throckmorton, and Barnstone, http://www.earlychristianwritings.com/text/gospelhebrews-throck.html

It may also relate to the foot-washing episode in John 13 where Jesus removes "his garments," knowing he "is going to God." Acts 7 mentions the "garments of the witnesses" laid at the feet of Saul during the stoning of Stephen, an episode from Luke that Dr. Eisenman has shown bears many details in common with the stoning of James. These details from Hebrew Matthew are important ties to the overwritten canonical betrayal character, James the Just, showing affinity not only with the character Judas, but to Jesus as well.

Hebrew Matthew has a heavenly Mary, not an earthly one. The "virgin birth" was originally a spiritual concept:

(Cyril of Jerusalem, Discourse on Mary Theotokos 12a): It is written in the Gospel of the Hebrews: When Christ wished to come upon the earth to men, the good Father summoned a mighty power in Heaven, which was called Michael, and entrusted Christ to the care thereof. *And the power came into the world and it was called Mary*, and Christ was in her womb seven months.

Crawford S. Griffin, Judas Iscariot, Author of the Fourth Gospel

In 1892, Crawford S. Griffin proposed the intriguing thesis that Judas Iscariot was the beloved disciple, and author of the fourth, or John's, Gospel. In John 13:23–28, Peter is asking the "disciple whom Jesus loved" to ask Jesus to tell them who it was who would betray him. Jesus answers that it is "the one to whom I shall give the morsel when I have dipped it." The author of the Gospel says it was given to Judas. Verse 27 says Jesus said to him, "What you are going to do, do quickly"; then verse 28 says, "but no one at the table knew why he said this to him." Presumably Judas knew, as the one being spoken to, so the only disciple whom this "beloved disciple" could have been was Judas. Although widely acknowledged now among experts on John that chapter 21, with John as "beloved disciple," is a later addition, Griffin concluded that the author of the Gospel must have been Judas, the "beloved disciple."[68]

---

[68]   C.S. Griffen, 1892, http://archive.org/stream/judasiscariotaut00grif#page/n3/ mode/2up.

Apocryphal Books of Enoch

Enoch is a savior according to 2 Enoch; Moses and Samuel are saviors according to 3 Enoch:

> For you [Enoch] shalt be glorified before the Lord's face for all time, since the Lord chose you, rather than all men on earth, and designated you writer of all his creation, visible and invisible, *and redeemed of the sins of man,* and helper of your household (2 Enoch 64:5).

> But when the Holy One, blessed be He, sees, that there is no righteous man in the generation, and no pious man on earth, and no justice in the hands of men; *and [that there is] no man like unto Moses, and no intercessor as Samuel who could pray before MAQOM for the salvation and for the deliverance,* and for His Kingdom, that it be revealed in the whole world; *and* for His great Right Hand that He put it before Himself again *to work great salvation by it* for Israel (3 Enoch 48:5).

The Dead Sea Scrolls

The "pierced Messiah" text—4Q285, fragment 7, "The Book of War"—a part of the Qumran collection of Dead Sea Scrolls from the deserts of Jordan, became a brief sensation in November, 1991, when Dr. Eisenman and Michael Wise announced its discovery.[69] In it, Eisenman said he found what he claimed to be an indication that the martyred- Messiah tradition was a Judaic one as well as a Christian one, and thus was not unique to Christianity. But as Geza Vermes said in his collection of scrolls translations, it is "Messiah piercing," not "Messiah pierced" (Hebrew "hmytw," line 4, fragment 4): "I ['thy Name'] will strike your bow..." and fragment 7, "the Prince of the Congregation, the Branch of David (the Righteous Teacher) will kill

---

69   Robert Eisenman, The Dead Sea Scrolls and the First Christians.

him by strikes and by wounds." Again, the context is one of a disciple being "struck" by the Master and made fit for divine union: "sacrifice the man" and "Strike, O Shepherd." The whole Messianic final battle idea that is so prominent in the Scrolls milieu (The War Scroll, for example) has nothing to do with any worldly war, but takes place within the disciple between the lower self and the Spirit—the drive to merge into the God-self. The highly stylized array of battalions, with seven of this and twelve of that, is obviously a symbolic battle, not a flesh-and-blood battle among nations. The John 18:37 "piercing" of Christ is a similar misunderstanding of the Hebrew, in this case of Zechariah 12:10. The Hebrew is "daqaru," or idiomatic, "reviled." The people were not reviling 'him'—that is another mistranslation—but "Me," the Lord. They "shall mourn over it [not 'him']." See Chatbible. com, Zechariah 12:10 notes.

The preeminent Dead Sea Scrolls expert is Dr. Robert Eisenman. This one lapse is no reason to discount his incredible achievement in putting the Pesherim (Commentaries) into proper context in the first century, not BCE, and identifying Paul as the "Spouter of Lying," Ananus as the "Wicked Priest," and James as the first-century "Righteous Teacher."[69] All he lacks is an appreciation for the living Masters tradition: the "Sons of Man," Community Rule III:13–14 are Masters. Also: "His Holy Name" (The Damascus Document 43(20) and 57(34)) isn't Yahweh, but the Apophasis Logos—the Word, or Shabd.

The Qur'an

The 'weighty' Word is Eastern mystic Shabd, in common with Christian tradition, and the recitation, "to pray", is the Eastern 'simran,' for concentration. Nighttime is the best for performing devotions. Some translations say a "Message" will be sent in place of "a weighty Word."

Surah 73:1–5

SurahAl-Muzzammil (The Shrouded One)

[Shakir 73:1] O you who have wrapped up in your garments!

[Shakir 73:2] Rise to pray in the night except a little,

[Yusufali 73:3] Half of it, or a little less,

[Yusufali 73:4] Or a little more; and recite the Qur'an in slow, measured rhythmic tones.

[Shakir73:5] Surely We will make to light upon you a weighty Word.

Conclusion

No scholar in the world presently understands the Gospel of Judas at all. Of the twenty-one scholars reporting to the First International Conference on the Gospel of Judas[70] and the twenty-nine scholars creating the twenty-eight reports to the Proceedings of the International Congress on the Tchacos Codex[71], not even one rightly perceives that the one sacrificing the "man who bears me" *is Judas sacrificing himself,* and not Jesus.

There is no reason to think that the New Testament canon is the original text of the story of the first-century Master, Jesus Christ. Elaine Pagels wrote, "Today, New Testament scholars differ in judgment about what and how much in the gospels is based on actual history."[72] There are other provably early competing storylines that don't support the New Testament Jesus story. The Gospel of Thomas, for example --a sayings record-- is widely regarded as the earliest and most primitive form of Gospel. This Gnostic author has James the Just in an elevated role not exceeded even by Jesus himself: "the one for whom *heaven and earth were created."* One does not need to know a word of Coptic to understand that the text the scholarly team at National Geographic translated for the Gospel of Judas has a sacrificed Judas. The "man who bears" Jesus, who is to be tormented, are the baptized in his Name, and Judas "exceeds" even them as the one to sacrifice "the man who bears" Jesus. He is to be "replaced" by his gnostic Master Jesus, spiritually, so that the former man—the old elements that made up "Judas"—can return to their original place of repose in lower heavenly realms while

---

70   Madeleine Scopello, ed., The Gospel of Judas in Context.

71   April DeConick, ed., The Codex Judas Papers.

72   Karen King and Elaine Pagels, Reading Judas (Viking, New York, 2007).

he returns to his almighty God, as every mystic aspires to do. The lines about Judas seeing a "vision" of his stoning *at the hands of fellow disciples*, as was known to have happened to only James, show that Judas was really James the Just. "The Gospel of Judas clearly depicts Jesus' death as a sacrifice," Johanna Brankaer noted in DeConick's report[73] This is the problem. It is all about scholarly religious bias and ignorance. Self-sacrifice is readily apparent in mystic writings, but it seems not to be on their radar—or on anybody's radar. It is time now to fix that.

So what does this say about Jesus? Maybe that Jesus was not a real person? What is wrong with reading the New Testament as the literature— not history—that it is? It takes a retired farmer from Hawaii to tell the Ph.D.s that "Judas" is not Judas and that Jesus is not the sacrifice that we all thought that he was? That other key players in the narrative were pure inventions? Shouldn't the Ph.D.s be the ones telling *us*? That is their *job*. As long as scholars look, as hard as they might try, all the papers and books that they throw at this will not change the conclusion that Judas was fictional, Jesus didn't die for anyone, and that James was the real savior. Furthermore, James was one of a long series of saviors which didn't begin with him nor end with him. This is the only consistently workable solution to understanding all the sources now available. Jesus and Judas are inventions of clever writers of the first century to make James disappear from history for the selfish ends of a few. The ruse worked beyond the wildest dreams of those responsible for its creation. The result, unfortunately, is that millions who have thought that they were saved were not, that millions today who think they are saved are not, and that millions more will come to think that they are saved and will not be so. This is not about any religion! There is no intent here to convert. There is nothing to convert to. Only living Masters can save.[74]

And Masters are beyond religion.[75] They are from above the seven heavens, not restricted by any literature that would try to mold them.

73   DeConick, The Codex Judas Papers, 391.

74   Swami Ji, Sar Bachan, bachan # 53, 55.

75   Julian Johnson, The Path of the Masters (Radha Soami Satang Beas, Beas, India, 1939), 202.

These teachings have been the same all along. They pertain strictly to mystic practice and not to literary fiction, outward ritual, or anyone's "manifold dogma." It is everyone's birth right to put them to the test. This is the true path to salvation. Right now, with the three Abrahamic religions, what we have is literature, not a way out.

Biblical scholars will make no further progress on the Gospel of Judas or on any other New Testament-related documents without appreciating the mystic story that is overwritten in both. The New Testament is disinformation, at least as used by the church; that is, any orthodox reading and understanding of the Gospels and Acts, as if they represent something approaching history. They most decidedly *do not*. Gnosticism is informative, orthodoxy is disinformative. The Gnostics didn't thwart orthodoxy. They didn't need to. The Gnostics had the high ground and were just trying to set the record straight when they wrote their Gospels and Apocalypses. Their scripture was the Jewish scriptures, not the New Testament Gospels. Their Masters, it is clear, didn't start and end with Jesus Christ. Seth was a central figure for many; James was a towering figure. Peter—and even Philip, Mary, and the others—were apparently destined for Mastership. In fact, their Jesus may have been the same as Paul's: the heavenly redeemer, the Holy Spirit, the divine Logos. Jesus only walked and talked his way through gnostic teachings so far as necessary to address the misconceptions spawned by the New Testament Gospels. Isn't it time to see past the hype and propaganda?

If there is one thing this author has learned from engaging with academia as an outsider, it is this: there is little curiosity among academic professionals for new sources of information that are not normative— that is, from within academia. Some avenue to academia must be made available to nonacademics who have something to offer. This is a matter of firsthand experience for this author and a repeatedly bitter one. There is an entire universe of information that academics are not privy to and should be. Look to India. Go there. There is spiritual greatness in timeless India. Some types of knowing can only be experienced firsthand, not learned from the tired, old, well-trodden paths between ivy towers. This writer will never forget the moment of recognition the first time Judas came into focus as "the sacrifice." This stunning revelation is meant for everyone! Here is a call for bridging East to West. Dr. Bart Ehrman has said, "What we need in religious discussion is a frank and brutally honest sharing of views, not simply an insistence that everyone comes to believe, or disbelieve, what we do."[76] Well, Dr. Ehrman, here is sharing. The obvious story making, scripture hijacking, and quote mining that passes for history is no longer acceptable. We have the modern mystic teachings of the East! Why do scholars not know of them? Here is a start for you: Science of the Soul.org.

Just because one may be unfamiliar with Eastern mysticism and its detailed teachings is no reason to reject it out of hand. If one is not comfortable with doctrines as seemingly foreign as karma and reincarnation, be sure that these are taught in the Bible.[77] Jesus himself says, "He is Elijah" when asked about John. "Go and sin no more, *lest a worse thing* come unto thee" (John 5:14) refers to *karma.*

One can see from what has been presented here that fundamental concepts are in evidence in all sources: the Word, the Master, salvation by practice or works. The last is seen in "Not everyone who says to me, 'Lord, Lord,' shall enter the kingdom of heaven, *but he who does* the will of my Father who is in heaven" (Matt. 7:21, italics added). Only the New Testament Gospels say anything about God giving up a martyred child to save others. Any other scripture said to be such a sacrifice found between the covers of the "Holy Bible" is a misreading of said scripture. Sacrifice, particularly human sacrifice, is a barbaric concept born in another time and place and thankfully is out of step with modern sensibilities.

In just fifty years, the world will have spent two millennia under the shadow of a morbid interpretation of God's will for us. God hates sacrifice! Does not Hosea 6:6 tell us so? So He kills His own son? What

76   Bart Ehrman, Misquoting Jesus (Harper Collins, New York, 2005), 249.

77   Stone, Mystic Bible, 217.

about those who were born to die *before* Jesus lived? Did they die in vain? Does any of it make any sense at all? We can use these final few years of the second millennium to see that the third millenium does not take us even further down this dark alley. Jesus didn't write the New Testament, and he surely would be appalled by what is there, if he were real and here today. Better to read what a real Master—James—taught. At least he is attested to historically. His message is one of light and life, not one based upon his death, or anyone else dying. What a tragedy that his life of light was used as the model for a cult of death!

This book may or may not be appreciated right away. It could be fifty, or even a hundred years, before the readings brought to light here are understood as correct, or even useful. But given the pace of biblical discoveries and dissemination even in recent history, that is to be expected—however unfortunate it is. One hopes that biblical scholars will quickly pick up on the fact that Judas is the sacrifice—not Jesus—and what that means for the Gospel of Judas, the other Gnostic texts, and the Bible. In time, this radical view of Judas as a Master and a sacrifice will be a given. It isn't a question of if, but when. *No further progress in New Testament study is possible until this report is recognized as true.* It *will* be the standard in due time. Neither the Judas consensus scholars nor the revisionists are correct.

This short work isn't the last word, even on Judas. It is merely to point to the Path that underlies all paths. There is still much to learn, and this is a call for help to do it. Could the Coptic presently rendered for "fornicate in my Name" actually be the more neutral "engage in my Name"? "Then they will fornicate in my name" – as most translators have it – makes no sense. These are, after all, the Adamic souls, the "races of angels," that Jesus is talking about at page 54, line 25. Jenott says that the "first star" should be Judas, their leader. And we know now that he is a good guy. The Adamic races will perhaps "slay their desires ['offspring'], and [forsake] wickedness" (54:26-55:1). This is really just the beginning. There is much left to discover in this fascinating puzzle of the New Testament and its Gnostic progenitors. The Gospels weren't written to give up their secrets easily, but with the Gnostic and Qumran discoveries of recent times, and the growing strength of the mythicist argument, we are in a better position than ever to learn them. Let's hope that soon we will learn them all and finally see the whole picture of the first century as it really happened. Only then will we be able to forge ahead together into a more informed and enlightened future for us all.

Summary

Proof from the Gnostic texts that James was 'Judas' – both sacrifice and Master

The Apocryphon of James (NHC I, 2)

"Woe to those who have seen the Son [of] Man;" (3:17-18) > "Woe to that man by whom the Son of man is betrayed ['delivered']" (Mark 14:21) "blessed will they be who have not consorted with the man, and they who have not consorted with him, and they who have not spoken with him" (3:19-22) >"sacrifice the man" (Gospel of Judas 56:21)

"that, when I [Jesus] have come, I might ascend (again)" (14:40) > "and again he came ... Rise, let us be going" (Mark 14:40-42)

"But pay heed to the glory that awaits me" (14:26) > "When he [Judas] had gone out, Jesus said 'Now is the Son of man glorified.'" (John 13:31)

"I [Jesus] shall depart from you ... I shall strip myself" (14:33-35) > "a young man [James] followed him ... and fled naked" (Mark 14:51-52)

"And I [James] pray that the beginning may come from you [his fellow disciples], for thus I shall be capable of salvation, since they [the disciples' disciples] will be enlightened through me" (16:14-15) > "and he touched his ear and healed him" (Luke 22:51. Also John 18:9-11. Malchus is initiated by "one of those"/"one of them"/"Peter" [James], illustrating in the canon the Apocryphon of James dynamic of mastership succession.

"Touching *the right ear*" struck by the symbolic sword of the Word is spiritually healing for "*him*.")

Proof from the Gnostic Apocalypses that Judas was James in the Canonical Inversions:

Compare the inversions in the canonical Betrayal of the Apocalypses of James with the inversion of Jamesian purity observances in the Dead Sea Scrolls of Pauline theology (see Dr. Robert Eisenman). The "betrayal" happens in the Gospels and in Acts 1 just when a successor to Jesus would be expected to be chosen. The "traitor" Judas in the canonical Gospels is really James the Just, successor Master to Jesus in the Gnostic Apocalypses of James, inverted tendentiously to hide his coming.

First Apocalypse of James, NHC V, 3 (excerpt 30:15–33:10: the heart of the betrayal original parallels)

http://gnosis.org/naghamm/1ja.html
http://www.scribd.com/doc/13561147/The-Apocalypse-of-James-Aocalypsis-Anabathmoi-Iacobi-Ascents-of-James-brother-of-Jesus

"When James heard of his suffering and was much distressed, they awaited the sign of his coming. And he came after several days. And James was walking upon the mountain which is called 'Gaugelan', with his disciples, who listened to him because they had been distressed, and he was [...] a comforter, saying, 'This is[...] second [...]' Then the crowd dispersed, but James remained [...] prayer [...], as was his custom.

"And the Lord appeared to him. Then he stopped (his) prayer and embraced him. He kissed him, saying, 'Rabbi, I have found you! I have heard of your sufferings, which you endured. And I have been much distressed. My compassion you know. Therefore, on reflection, I was wishing that I would not see this people. They must be judged for these things that they have done. For these things that they have done are contrary to what is fitting.'

"The Lord said, 'James, do not be concerned for me or for this people. I am he who was within me. Never have I suffered in any way, nor have I been distressed. And this people has done me no harm. But this (people) existed as a type of the archons, and it deserved to be destroyed through them. But[…]the archons, […] who has […] but since it […] angry with […] The just […] is his servant. Therefore your name is "James the Just". You see how you will become sober when you see me. And you stopped this prayer. Now since you are a just man of God, you have embraced me and kissed me. Truly I say to you that you have stirred up great anger and wrath against yourself. But (this has happened) so that these others might come to be.'

"But James was timid (and) wept. And he was very distressed. And they both sat down upon a rock. The Lord said to him, 'James, thus you will undergo these sufferings. But do not be sad. For the flesh is weak. It will receive what has been ordained for it. But as for you, do not be timid or afraid'. The Lord ceased.

"Now when James heard these things, he wiped away the tears in his eyes and very bitter […] which is […]. The Lord said to him, 'James, behold, I shall reveal to you your redemption. When you are seized, and you undergo these sufferings, a multitude will arm themselves against you that they may seize you. And in particular three of them will seize you—they who sit (there) as toll collectors.'"

Connecting verses from the Gnostic Apocalypses of James to the New Testament narrative showing that Judas was James in the Canonical Inversions:

First Apocalypse of James

"I have given you a sign" (NHC 24:10) "gave them a sign" [the "kiss"] (Matt. 26:48).

"Cup of bitterness to the sons of light" (25:15) "let this cup pass from me" (Matt. 26:39).
"This is the second Master" (30:25) "Those who seek enter through you" (Second Apoc. 55:1) "I know whom I have chosen." (John 13:18).

"Then the disciples dispersed, but James remained in prayer" (30:25) "he withdrew and prayed" (Luke 22:41).

"I am he who was within me" (31:15) "I know whom I have chosen" and "I am he" (John 13:18–19).

"You will undergo suffering" (32:15) "he began to be sorrowful and troubled" (Matt. 26:37).

"You are aware and stopped this prayer" (32:5) "Sit here while I pray" (Matt. 26:36).

"The flesh is weak" (32:20) "the flesh is weak" (Matt. 26:41).

"It will receive what has been ordained for it" (32:20) "thy will be done" (Matt. 26:42).

Jesus "comes" three times (Matt. 26:40–44) Peter's three denials (reversed in Matt. 26:70 from Apoc. Peter, following).

"You have embraced and kissed me" (32:5) "He said 'Hail Master!' and kissed him" (Matt. 26:49).

"A multitude will arm themselves against you" (33:5) "band of soldiers

102

with weapons" (John 18:3, Mark 14:43).

"Seize you" (33:5) "seized him" (Matt. 26:48, 50, John 18:12).

"In particular, three of them will seize you" (33:5) "a band of soldiers, their captain, and their officers seized Jesus" (John 18:12) "chief priests, scribes and elders" (Mark 14:43, Luke 22:52).
"When you come into their power, their guard will call to you" (33:13–14) "Whom do you seek?" They answered him, "Jesus of Nazareth." (John 18:4–5).

"You are to say to him, 'I AM a son, and I AM from the Father.'" (33:16–17) "I am he." (John 18:6).

Second Apocalypse of James (V,4)

"I am he [twice] who was first summoned by the Great One ... who stripped himself and went about naked" (2 Apoc. 46:15) "I am he." (John 18:8), "stripped him, put his own clothes on him" (Matt. 27:31).

"As a brother was he sought" (46:20) "Whom do you seek?" (John 18:7).

"For just as you are the first, having clothed yourself, you are the first who will strip himself" (2 Apoc. 56:10).

"He is the one who will come. He will provide an ending for what has begun and a beginning for what is about to end. He was the virgin, stripped and rising naked" (2 Apoc. 58:10–20),
Compare all the above from 2 Apocalypse of James with:

"And a young man followed him, with nothing but a linen cloth about his body, and they seized him, but he left the linen cloth and fled naked" (Mark 14:51–2) and "stripped him, and led him away to crucify him" (Matt. 27:31).

"Hail my brother, hail!" (2 Apoc.50:10/CT32:5) "Hail, Master!" (Matt. 26:49).

"Bring me from a tomb alive" (2 Apoc. 63:5) "He is not here, for he has risen," "risen from the dead," and "tomb" (Matt. 28:6–8).

In most cases in these parallel occurrences, the order is roughly the same: the sign, the bitter cup, prayer "on a rock," "the flesh is weak," "thy will," "what is ordained," "Hail!" and then the kiss, an "armed multitude" coming (John 18), "naked" and "fleeing" (Mark 14).

Apocalypse of Peter, VII, 3:72: "He [Jesus] was about to reprove you [Peter] three times in this night."

Apocalypse of Peter, first paragraph, about inner vision of Jesus—inverted in the four Gospels: Peter denying Jesus a third time is in all four gospels, and this after Jesus comes three times and finds them "sleeping." in this night. (They are actually trying to meditate, and he tells Peter his concentration is not complete.) Three pieces are the same: the denial, three times, and "in this night". This can't be coincidental. It comes just after the three times "coming" to them.

"Crowning" (71:30) "Soldiers plaited a crown of thorns" (John 19:2).

Gospel of Judas:

Passover setting in both texts. Main character "walking" and "twelve disciples" called.

"Apophasis Logos" is "Word" in John 1.

Anami Desh (Sant Mat's "No name region" – see *Sar Bachan*) is "region never called by any name" (47:13).

"You will be replaced by someone" (36:1). Matthias isn't mentioned as he is in Acts 1. This is Jesus merging into him.

"You will not be able to go there but will grieve a great deal" (35:20) "woe to the one who delivers me" (Matt. 26:24).

"You will be replaced by someone in order that the twelve [*elements*] may again come to completion in their god." (36:1–3) "I tell you this now before it takes place; so that when it does take place you will believe that I am he."(John 13:19).
"For your sake they will reign and will become Kings" (2 Apoc. 56:5), "generation with no King" (Gospel of Judas 53:24).

"You stirred up wrath against yourself" (1 Apoc.32:10), "Your wrath has been kindled" (56:23—shows Judas is James).

"You will exceed them all, you will sacrifice the man that bears me" (56:20), "woe to that man who delivers me" (Matt. 26:24). This is *Judas* sacrificing himself; the "woe to that man" is his sacrifice!

This climax passage is in answer to "What will those who have been baptized in your Name do?" (55:23–25) Next line: "Tomorrow they will torment the one who bears me," followed by "You will exceed them all, for you will sacrifice the man who bears me" (56:20–21)—no change in subject! The tradition in the Gnostic version preceded the canon, there is no Matthias in the Gospel of Judas. The above are just the most obvious parts. There are others that are not so obvious. Other Gnostic texts, such as Thomas the Contender, detail meditation technique, like the Apocalypse of Peter does right after the three denials of Peter.

Aside from Charles Hedrick stating that the Second Apocalypse of James is early because of lack of allusions to New Testament traditions, the passage, "Hail, my brother, my brother, hail" changed to "Hail, Master!" shows the canon is later and is meant to accommodate the late orthodox virgin-birth development.

Any two of these above would identify the parallel tradition, and the Gnostics would *not* copy an orthodox tradition of sacrifice, especially of humans, and certainly not *ever* the Master as sacrifice.

The Acts 1 replacement of Matthias has "Judas" in place of James (from Clement's Pseudoclementine Recognitions 1:70 James "falling headlong" off the Temple wall, thrown by Paul). Acts 1:18, has Judas "falling headlong" to his suicidal death (not hanging as in Matthew).

Joseph Barsabbas *Justus* covers James *the Just* as the "defeated" candidate (Acts 1:23).

The election (by lots, from Acts 1) is for "episcopate of Jerusalem" (from church fathers); Acts 1:20 says, "his office let another take," but being an Apostle is not an office: "episcopate" is.

John 13:18 is James. Taken from Psalm41:9, the Douay Rheims translation, comes "Even my own kinsman, the one who ate my bread, has greatly supplanted me." The Hebrew root for "heel" is "aqab" and has the root letters for "Yacov," Hebrew for the Greek "Jacob" or English "James." This replacement dynamic is the meaning of the idiomatic Hebrew, not the literal, "lifted his heel against me" as some sort of attack. The negative connotation of "supplant" fits the negative view that the orthodox Gospel writers would have had against a successor. It just so happened that, in a bit of serendipity, the idiomatic "lifted his heel against me" fit so well into the tendentious inversion. John probably knew all this and was just making a clever linguistic sleight-of-hand.

Also, the Gospel According to the Hebrews—now lost but mentioned by a number of first-century church fathers—has Jesus giving the bread to James, not the disciples (Matt. 26) not to "them" (Mark 14 and Luke 22), and not to Judas (John 13). Bread is a symbol of life, not death.

In Hegesippus, James is said to utter, "Father forgive them for they know not what they do" and "You will see the Son of man coming with power and on the clouds of heaven." Both quotes are given to Jesus in the New Testament narrative.

Luke 11:1 has the Lord's prayer taught by John to *his disciples*. That John *had* disciples shows that he was a Master in his own right.

The Gospel of Thomas 12 has the disciples told to "Go to James, for whom heaven and earth were created." Another passage in Hebrew Matthew has John as savior of the world at 17:11. Only the New Testament has Jesus as savior, but no mention of James or John as saviors, which they were in many extra-biblical sources and in Sant Mat (www.rssb.org/ScienceoftheSoul.org).

Bibliography

Brown, Francis. *Brown-Driver-Briggs Hebrew and English Lexicon.* Hendrickson Publishers, Peabody, MA, 2012.

DeConick, April D. *The Thirteenth Apostle.* Continuum, New York, 2007.

DeConick, April, ed. *The Codex Judas Papers.* E. J. Brill, Leiden, The Netherlands, 2008.

Ehrman, Bart D. *The Orthodox Corruption of Scripture.* Oxford University Press, New York, 1993.

Ehrman, Bart. D. *Misquoting Jesus.* Harper Collins, New York, 2005.

Ehrman, Bart. D. *The Lost Gospel of Judas Iscariot.* Oxford University Press, New York, 2006.

Eisenman, Robert. *The Dead Sea Scrolls and the First Christians.* Castle Books, Edison, NJ, 1996.

Eisenman, Robert. *James the Brother of Jesus.* Penguin Books, New York, 1998.

Eisenman, Robert. *The New Testament Code.* Viking, New York, 1997.

Eusebius. *History of the Church.* Translated by G.A. Williamson. Penguin Books, New York, 1989.

Helms, Randel. *Gospel Fictions*. Prometheus Books, Amherst, New York, 1988.

Jenott, Lance. *The Gospel of Judas*. Mohr Siebeck, Tubingen, Germany, 2011.

Johnson, Julian P. *The Path of the Masters*. Radha Soami Satang Beas, Beas, India, 1939.

King, Karen l. and Elaine Page ls. *Reading Judas*. Viking, New York, 2007.

Klassen, William. *Judas, Betrayer or Friend of Jesus?* Fortress Press, Augsberg Fortress, Minneapolis, MN, 1996.

Kloppenborg, John. *Q, the Earliest Gospel*. Westminster John Knox Press, Louisville, KY, 2008.

Meyer, Marvin. *The Gospel of Judas,* Wipf and Stock, Eugene, OR, 2011.

Meyer, Marvin, Rodolphe Kasser, and Gregor Wurst. *The Gospel of Judas,* 2nd ed. National Geographic Society, Washington, D.C., 2006.

Pervo, Richard. *The Mystery of Acts*. Polebridge Press, Santa Rosa, CA, 2008.

Robinson, James M., ed. *The Nag Hammadi Library*. E. J. Brill, Leiden, The Netherlands, 1978.

Scopello, Madeleine, ed. *The Gospel of Judasin Context*. E. J. Brill, Leiden, The Netherlands, 2006.

Singh, Charan. *Die to Live*. Radha Soami Satsang Beas, Beas, India, 1979.

Singh, Charan. *Lighton St. John*. Radha Soami Satsang Beas, Beas, India, 1967.

Stone, Randolph. *Mystic Bible*. Radha Soami Satsang Beas, Beas, India, 1956.

Swami Ji Maharaj. *Sar Bachan*. Radha Soami Sasang Beas, Beas, India, 1964.

Wahler, Robert. *The Bible Says "Saviors"—Obadiah 1:21*. Xlibris, Bloomington, IN, 2009.

Wells, G.A. *The Historical Evidence for Jesus*, Prometheus Books, Amherst, NJ, 2008.

Online Book Club

What if someone provided proof that our long-held beliefs about Jesus of Nazareth were incorrect? Author Robert Wahler is attempting to do just that with his 2016 non-fiction book, Misreading Judas: How Biblical Scholars Missed the Biggest Story of All Time. The author's thesis offers a new interpretation of the relationship between Jesus and Judas. Wahler asserts the story of Judas was not a betrayal and sacrifice of Jesus at all but rather a self-sacrifice by Judas as part of the Gnostic tradition called mastership succession. The author's research holds both Jesus and Judas in a very different light from that of orthodox religious teachings. Could Jesus really have been merely one in a succession of many spiritual Masters?

The Gnostic Gospel of Judas was likely composed by second-century Gnostic Christians. The surprisingly intact papyrus containing the text first surfaced publicly in 1970. It reveals conversations between Jesus and Judas Iscariot. Wahler claims no one has correctly translated the Gospel of Judas until his research emerged. He faults the Christian scholars who initially interpreted the text, saying they were ignorant to the Gnostic orientation necessary to adequately understand the ancient writings. In Eastern spiritual traditions, mysticism is the practice of spiritual knowing (gnosis) through meditation and other vehicles for merging with Spirit. A longtime student of Eastern mysticism, Wahler insists the story of Judas and all of the Gnostic Gospels must be interpreted through the lens of mysticism.

In addition to Gnostic texts and the New Testament, Wahler's comparative analysis draws from the work of Eastern spiritual teacher Maharaj Charan Singh. From this viewpoint, Wahler contends when Jesus tells Judas to "sacrifice the man who bears me," he is referring to a mystical sacrifice, not the physical sacrifice of Jesus. In the mystical interpretation, Jesus is telling Judas that he (Judas) will sacrifice his individual self to become one with his spiritual Master. This form of self-sacrifice is a traditional practice by the Gnostics of that time. In addition, the author asserts that Judas is the same person as the lesser-known apostle, James the Just. If they are one in the same, according to Wahler, then the Judas-as-betrayer story was a cover for what really happened: James (Judas) succeeded Jesus as Master.

Robert Wahler maintains that the mystical self-sacrifice by Judas, and his subsequent mastership, was misinterpreted and "inverted" by biblical scholars to hide the uncomfortable truth that other great Masters preceded and succeeded Jesus. The simple existence of a succession of Masters through self-sacrifice challenges the conventional knowledge of Jesus' role in history. Wahler is not saying that Jesus wasn't a prophet and great spiritual Master. He is saying Jesus wasn't the only one and that he didn't die for anyone's sins. Wahler challenges, "There is no reason to think that the New Testament canon is the original text of the story of the first-century Master, Jesus Christ."

For a relatively short book, 102 pages, Misreading Judas delivers volumes worth of sound comparative analysis. It is packed with quotations and line-by-line examination. I thought I might tire of the density but found I was fascinated by Wahler's methods and conclusions. Misreading Judas is not an easy read but is worth the effort. Some of the logic is complicated but at the same time convincing.

Wahler's writing is clear and easy to follow. The book's organization facilitates the reader's understanding of the material. Divided into four sections, the book traverses The Gospel of Judas, The Nag Hammadi Library, The New Testament, and resources on mystic readings of scriptures. Considering the complex punctuation required for the dense quotations, parenthetical and bracketed insertions, I was surprised that there were so few errors. The editor gave impeccable attention to precision in grammar and punctuation. A summary at the end of the book reviews the passages of text that directly support the thesis. Both the summary and Wahler's concluding remarks help to connect the dots. Note: In deference to Eastern mysticism, Robert Wahler capitalizes the word "Master" in his book. I have done the same for consistency.

Wahler is not entirely alone in his progressive positions. Some cursory research on my part revealed that there is growing consensus among religious scholars for Wahler's view of Judas as beloved and obedient disciple, rather than betrayer. The author's belief in the succession of Masters is, however, another story. This is where he is out on a limb. Save non-Christians and very progressive theologians, support for this conclusion is less enthusiastic, to be sure.

I rate Misreading Judas: How Biblical Scholars Missed the Biggest Story of All Time 4 out of 4 stars. If you are open-minded and are interested in biblical history or Eastern mysticism, I think you will be fast captivated by this book. If you are outraged by Wahler's conclusions, you might enjoy being engaged in what can only be described as the debate of the millennia.

- Eva Darrington, Online Book Club

Foreword Reviews

This energetic work serves as a beguiling introduction to gnosticism. If a Dan Brown novel were turned into a dizzying, real-life unraveling of a newly revealed gnostic text, it might read something like Robert Wahler's Misreading Judas, a heady nonfiction tractate that attempts nothing less than a complete upheaval of traditional Christian exegesis.

Considering the scope of the work, the book, which is divided into four sections, is surprisingly short. Wahler, a lay researcher and writer, relishes in his "outsider" status, taking aim at both Christian orthodoxy and academic orthodoxy. In his introduction, he outlines his ultimate mission: proving that the biblical story of Judas was never a literal betrayal of Jesus but actually a description of the gnostic tradition of mastership succession and self-sacrifice.

To make this case, the book examines The Gospel of Judas, which was first translated in 2006 by the National Geographic Society, as well as selections from the Nag Hammadi Library, a collection of gnostic texts discovered in Egypt in 1945. The book also examines various passages of the New Testament in light of these new gnostic readings.

Misreading Judas's energetic, investigative tone is at first alluring, though it becomes frenetic, puzzling, and hard to follow. Source excerpts are crammed together in long, uninterrupted litanies, with only brief, intermittent explications. The book succeeds where the sourcing is less indulgent, less tangential, and better layered into clearer, more authoritative conclusions.

The fervent tone also contributes to moments of presumption. The book's conclusion dismisses modern-day Christians as dupes misled by corrupt institutions, and simultaneously elevates its own status to that of a heroic sage. "It isn't a question of if, but when," the book speculates on its own importance to religious scholarship. "No further progress in New Testament study is possible until this report is recognized as true. It will be the standard in due time."

Such proclamations detract from the book's strengths. Misreading

Judas serves as a beguiling introduction to gnosticism. The strongest passages detail the esoteric history of the spiritual movement, and the personal nature of mysticism. The book astonishingly connects Judas and Jesus's spiritual practices to Eastern mysticism in India. In striving to locate Eastern precedents in Abrahamic religions, the book offers interesting and novel perspectives on biblical narratives, such as the influence of karmic cycles in the New Testament.

Misreading Judas may prove too busily written and thematically arcane for the uninitiated reader. On the other hand, those interested in history, theology, and philosophy will find more than enough to keep reading.

- Scott Neuffer - Foreword Reviews

Blue Ink Review

Is it possible that orthodox Christianity is based on a lie? For Robert Wahler, the answer is an unequivocal yes, an argument he pursues in his new book.

The evidence for this radical idea, the author notes, can be found in the Gospel of Judas. This recently rediscovered manuscript paints Judas, not as a betrayer, but as an heroic figure who carried out Jesus's orders that helped set in motion Christ's death and resurrection.

Wahler believes there's even more to this story: that this text needs to be read, not in light of modern Christian scholarship, but through the lens of Gnosticism (in which it was written) with a focus on Western and Eastern mysticism traditions. The author argues that the obscure manuscript provides evidence of bait and switch, namely that Judas was a stand-in, or alias, for James the Just, whom the author believes is the true successor of Christ (which undermines St. Paul's role in the development of the Church). Moreover, the text reveals hidden truths about the metaphysical nature of sacrifice and inner work that needs to be done to reach higher levels of consciousness.

This is all heady stuff, and for those not well versed in Gnostic thought, the author's exegesis of the text can be challenging. Yet, Wahler makes a valiant attempt to unpack the text, acting like a semiotics detective, exploring symbolism, and sometimes offering line-by-line commentary of ancient texts.

In his exuberance, however, Wahler's prose can turn dense and awkward, making his meaning hard to discern (e.g. : "The disciples ask that they be granted not to be tempted at 4:30, the same as Jesus tells them to 'watch and pray that you enter not into temptation.'").

As Wahler admits here, most scholars will balk at his claims. Still, the author's ideas are well-argued with citations, and while Misreading Judas sits outside the mainstream, it does provide an thought-provoking, if challenging, alternative look at Christianity.

Also available in hardcover and ebook.

- Blue Ink Review

U S. Review of Books

"Please, everyone, read the Gospel of Judas as the Gnostic text that it is. Stop importing a New Testament bias into it."

Lost for 1,700 years, the Gospel of Judas has an approximate origin in the 2nd century and was found preserved in an Egyptian cave. The Coptic language text was written by Gnostic Christians and elevates Judas from traitor to teacher of sacred mysteries. While this find has been touted as a great revelation, early Christians labeled it heresy.

Wahler defines self-sacrifice as the goal of Gnosticism. According to the book, when Jesus and Judas spoke together before the handover to Jewish leaders, their conversation concerned the personal sacrifice of Judas to become one with the Master. This would occur through the mystic practice of the Name (Logos, the presence of the divine). There is no mention of betrayal in this history. The author goes on to explain that a Gnostic Master is succeeded by the installation of another. Using New Testament text, he establishes the claim that the Apostle James became the Master following Jesus' death.

With the popularity of Dan Brown's pulse-racing books, including The Da Vinci Code, some who question the Christian interpretation of the New Testament gospels are now accepting the Gnostic viewpoint. Even the Jewish scholar Hyman Maccoby concurs in rejecting the idea of Judas as a traitor with Jewish involvement. This 103-page book is the author's call to fellow researchers of Biblical texts to join him in validating the Gospel of Judas' place in history. His own thorough research results are meticulously presented, comparing Nag Hammadi Library codes in Gnostic text to chapter and verse of Christian works to prove controversial points. Also included is a substantial bibliography.

- U. S. Review of Books (Reviewed by Donna Ford)

Kirkus Reviews

A revelatory interpretation of the Gospel of Judas.

In this book, Wahler (The Bible Says "Saviors," 2009) surveys the existing literature on an early gnostic Gospel that features Judas Iscariot as its main character, and he finds it lacking. He maintains that the Gospel's underlying narrative has been misread by biblical scholars, and he ascribes their errors to two main factors: a nearly unthinking deference to the orthodox New Testament texts (great chunks of which he dismisses as "Pauline propaganda"), and a scholarly ignorance of mystic gnostic traditions and their relationship to the canonical Gospels: "Is there no awareness in the ivy-covered academic halls of the long and storied tradition of the Eastern mystics?" he asks. Wahler provides an invaluable verse-by-verse close-reading of the Gospel of Judas and then widens his view to include other key works from the Nag Hammadi library of gnostic texts and, eventually, the canonical Gospels themselves. Along the way, he asks key questions, such as "who is this character, Judas? Is he the man that Paul never mentioned, the one he never knew, just like the Jesus he never knew?" Some of his answers to these questions are revolutionary ; for instance, he contends that the bulk of the New Testament amounts to a conscious coverup of the incendiary contents of the Judas Gospel, in which, he says, Judas essentially spiritually transforms from man to Messiah, supplanting Jesus. This is a comparatively short but densely packed exposition of a breadth of material that the Christian church has deemed apocryphal. Wahler offers readers very little in the way of introductory context, and many readers may wish that he'd slowed down at times to provide more explanatory information. However, his fellow experts will find thrilling, deep thought in these pages.

A tightly argued presentation of an explosive, Judas-centered counter-narrative.

-**Kirkus Reviews**